WORKING THEORY

**Recent Titles in
Series in Language and Ideology**

Literacy and Empowerment: The Meaning Makers
Patrick L. Courts

The Social Mind: Language, Ideology, and Social Practice
James Paul Gee

Eminent Rhetoric: Language, Gender, and Cultural Tropes
Elizabeth A. Fay

Transforming Mind: A Critical Cognitive Activity
Gloria Gannaway

Composition as a Cultural Practice
Alan W. France

WORKING THEORY

Critical Composition Studies for Students and Teachers

Judith Goleman

Foreword by Paulo Freire

Series in Language and Ideology
Edited by Donaldo Macedo

BERGIN & GARVEY
Westport, Connecticut • London

Library of Congress Cataloging-in-Publication Data

Goleman, Judith.
    Working theory : critical composition studies for students and
teachers / Judith Goleman ; foreword by Paulo Freire.
        p. cm. — (Series in language and ideology, ISSN 1069-6806)
    Includes bibliographical references (p.) and index.
    ISBN 0–89789–301–8 (hb : alk. paper). — ISBN 0–89789–302–6 (pb :
alk. paper)
      1. English language—Rhetoric—Study and teaching—Theory, etc.
2. English language—Composition and exercises—Theory, etc.
I. Title. II. Series.
PE1404.G64 1995
808'.042'07—dc20   94–40308

British Library Cataloguing in Publication Data is available.

Copyright © 1995 by Judith Goleman

All rights reserved. No portion of this book may be
reproduced, by any process or technique, without
the express written consent of the publisher.

Library of Congress Catalog Card Number: 94–40308
ISBN: 0–89789–301–8
      0–89789–302–6 (pbk.)
ISSN: 1069–6806

First published in 1995

Bergin & Garvey, 88 Post Road West, Westport, CT 06881
An imprint of Greenwood Publishing Group, Inc.

Printed in the United States of America

The paper used in this book complies with the
Permanent Paper Standard issued by the National
Information Standards Organization (Z39.48–1984).

P

> In order to keep this title in print and available to the academic community, this edition was produced using digital reprint technology in a relatively short print run. This would not have been attainable using traditional methods. Although the cover has been changed from its original appearance, the text remains the same and all materials and methods used still conform to the highest book-making standards.

Copyright Acknowledgments

The author and publisher are grateful for permission to reprint excerpts from the following copyrighted materials:

Louis Althusser and Etienne Balibar, *Reading Capital*. Trans. Ben Brewster. London: Verso, 1979.

M. M. Bakhtin, *The Dialogic Imagination: Four Essays*. Edited by Michael Holquist, translated by Michael Holquist and Caryl Emerson. Austin: University of Texas Press, 1981. Copyright © 1981. By permission of the University of Texas Press.

Thomas Newkirk, ed. *Only Connect: Uniting Reading and Writing*. Portsmouth, N.H.: Boynton/Cook, 1986. By permission of Thomas Newkirk.

"Reading, Writing, and the Dialectic Since Marx," reprinted by permission of Judith Goleman. In *Audits of Meaning: A Festschrift in Honor of Ann E. Berthoff* (Boynton/Cook Publishers Inc., Portsmouth, N.H., 1988).

For my husband, Neal Bruss
and
my daughter, Julia Goleman Bruss

Contents

Foreword by Paulo Freire		xi
Foreword by Donaldo Macedo		xiii
Acknowledgments		xxi
1	Working Theory: Introduction	1
2	Reading and Writing: Working the Dialectic since Marx	11
3	Toward Internally Persuasive Discourse Effects: Working Bakhtin's Theory of Language	43
4	Working the Relations between Academic Discourse and Subjectivity: A Cautionary Tale	63
5	How-to Hope in Stanley Fish: Foundationalism Reworked	93
Epilogue: Working the "Specific Reality of Discourse"		123
Works Cited		135
Index		139

Foreword

It is with great pleasure that I recommend to North American educators Judith Goleman's illuminating book, *Working Theory: Critical Composition Studies for Students and Teachers*. After reading *Working Theory*, readers will find it more difficult to allow themselves to be seduced by the temptation of dichotomies in which they lose themselves, preventing them from ever comprehending the world. In other words, theory–practice, popular knowledge–scientific knowledge, manual work–intellectual work, reading the word–reading the world are some of the "undichotomizables" that we often attempt to separate in a formal and mechanical manner.

Judith Goleman's *Working Theory* demonstrates beyond question that there is no way to underestimate or overestimate one or the other. That is to say, there is no way to reduce one to another for one implies the other in a necessary dialectical and contradictory relationship. The refusal of practitioners to engage in a theoretical reflection of their practice makes them unable to explain the raison d'être of relations among objects. Practice alone does not represent a theory about itself. But, without practice, theory runs the risk of wasting time, of diminishing both its own validity and the possibility of remaking itself. In the final analysis, theory and practice in their relationships, become naturally necessary as they complement each other. In this sense, there is always built into practice, a certain hidden theory or there is, in a theoretical project not born from a concrete practice, a future practice that will evaluate the theoretical hypothesis.

Working Theory speaks directly to the ever-present hidden theory in practice by effectively showing how to unveil practice in the sense of acquiring knowledge or recognizing in it the theory that is minimally or not yet perceived. Judith Goleman also challenges us to think about practice or theoretical task or theoretical practice. In other words, the real issue is how to discover in practice the vigor within which we approach reality, from the reality within which we act, that would give each time a more critical knowledge so we can arrive at the consciousness of the world. That is, the consciousness of the world is constituted in relation to the world, and it is not part of the self. Even though I run the risk of repeating what I have said many times in other writings, the world enables me to constitute the self in relation to *you*, the world. Then, the transformation of objective reality represents for me a form of writing reality. It is for this reason that I always insist that before learners attempt to learn how to read and write, they must read and write the world. They must comprehend the world that involves talk about the world. And when I speak of the world, I am not speaking exclusively about the nature of which I am a part—the trees, the animals, the mountains and rivers—but also of the social structures, politics, and culture in which I participate.

Judith Goleman's *Working Theory* is an indispensable reading: All educators will certainly agree that we cannot read the written word without the reading of the world that pushes us to rewrite the world, that is, to transform it.

—Paulo Freire

Foreword

Judith Goleman's book *Working Theory: Critical Composition Studies for Students and Teachers* is not only an excellent testimony of the ways in which theory informs practice but it is also a categorical statement that points to the inviability of the often false dichotomy between theory and practice. In reading *Working Theory*, I became more acutely aware of the dangers of the present theory phobia that characterizes the American academic culture, in general, and the field of composition, in particular. I was reminded of a serious conversation I had recently with Paulo Freire concerning the increasing anti-theory posture of many North American educators. He mentioned to me that in a conference in California a teacher got up and protested to him about his theoretical discourse: "Mr. Freire, how can you and Henry Giroux expect teachers to implement your liberatory pedagogy and empower students if they themselves feel so disempowered by the complexity of your theoretical discourse?" Paulo remarked to me that since the theory question is being raised more and more frequently, he was not surprised by the question, to which he had the following answer: "Look, if you don't understand Giroux, you obviously cannot understand me. If you don't understand me, it means that you cannot understand Sartre, you cannot understand Hegel, you cannot understand Marx, you cannot understand Althusser, you cannot understand Foucault and, my friend, if you cannot understand any of these great thinkers, I feel sorry for your students."

The understanding of this teacher's inability to see how theories systematically inform her practice cannot be achieved outside the ideological context that generates and shapes her practice to begin with. In other words, by deconstructing the ideological context so as to make the ideology bare, one begins to see clearly how the ever-present overdose of pragmatism functions to prevent the powerless students from "revers[ing] the distribution of power inscribed in texts by reinterpreting them from the subject-positions of those 'others,' excluded from the power by the reigning discursive authority."[1] This overdose of pragmatism—which characterizes the U.S. educational landscape—has led to the present onslaught of academics complaining about the complexity of a particular theoretical discourse because of its alleged lack of clarity. It is as if they have assumed that there is a "monodiscourse" that is characterized by its clarity and its availability to all. Judith Goleman, by espousing Bakhtin's philosophy of language, convincingly argues that at "any given moment in its historical exis-tence, language is heteroglot from top to bottom, stratified by different classes, races, genders, ages, professions, families, locales, and more." Therefore, given the polyphonic nature of our human community, one's consciousness is always informed—and shaped by—a multiplicity of competing discourses that in turn, contain competing and contradictory ideologies. As Goleman pointedly argues, "one's language, one's individual consciousness is always already saturated by the otherness of living language" since, according to Bakhtin, language "exists in other people's mouths, in other people's contexts, serving other people's intentions: it is from there that one must take the word, and make it one's own."

By denying oneself access to multiple discourses, including the theoretical discourse, the teacher at the conference in California not only is replicating a process in which she further de-skills herself but is also robbing her students of any possibility to develop the political clarity to understand the intricate and complex web of lies that function to reproduce the dominant ideology through traditional forms of literacy. Without political clarity, it is extremely difficult to understand one's historical and cultural positionality. However, political clarity can never be achieved if one accommodates a position of ambiguity that usually suppresses one's ideological contradictions: suppression is not only commonplace among many traditionalist educators; it is also a trait of many liberal educators who willfully fracture the intimate interrelationship between theory and practice.

To understand the ideological forms that lead to the fracturing of theory-practice, one must analyze the level of anti-intellectualism that permeates our culture, as evidenced by the denigration of any semblance of intellectualism. For instance, both President Bush and Vice President Dan Quayle made anti-intellectualism the hallmark of their campaign for the presidency, and it became the rallying cry of their subsequent administration. Cambridge, Massachusetts, with its high concentration of powerful institutions of higher education—such as Harvard and MIT—was presented by both Bush and Quayle as an example of what is wrong with America. The anti-intellectual culture prevents the development of a critical spirit that can engage in "challenging routine, unwilling mediocrity and clichés, asserting new scientific and unsentimental values."[2]

The essence of American anti-intellectualism is not only linked to the overdose of pragmatism that produces a constant disdain for any pursuit of theory, but it is also related to the universal intellectual typified in Julien Benda's "celebrated definition of intellectuals as a tiny band of super gifted and morally endowed philosopher-kings who constitute the conscience of mankind."[3] Accordingly, these "[r]eal intellectuals constitute a clergy, very rare creatures indeed, since what they uphold are eternal standards of truth and justice that are precise, not of this world . . . and whose activity is essentially not the pursuit of practical aims."[4] Thus, the universal intellectual imagined by Julien Benda has little relevance to practitioners in general, and practitioners of composition, in particular. It is for this reason that Judith Goleman correctly proposes Foucault's notion of the specific intellectual that is "relevant to the field of composition and its debate over the traditional role of the writing instructor as the master reader of students' truth-statements" and further provides the necessary intellectual tools to problematize the writing instructor's historical and privileged position as the master reader.

Foucault's proposal, which enables one to reconnect "the traditional transcendent values of knowledge and truth to worldly networks of power relations that are materialized in discourse," makes "everyone who works in any field connected either with the production or distribution of knowledge . . . an intellectual in Gramsci's sense."[5] Hence, a teacher or a composition instructor, by this very definition, cannot but consider himself or herself an intellectual whose "specific public role in society . . . cannot be reduced simply to being a faceless professional, a competent member of a class just going about her/his business."[6] The teacher, as an intellectual, "is an individual endowed with a faculty for representing, embodying, articulating a message, a view, an attitude, philosophy or opinion to, as well as for, a public."[7] Thus, a teacher as an intellectual cannot be reduced to a mere technicist who walks unreflexively through a labyrinth of procedures and methods that anesthetize students' critical ability in order to "domesticate social order for its self-preservation."[8] Accordingly, a teacher, as an intellectual, must reject pedagogical structures involving "practices by which one strives to domesticate consciousness, transforming it into an empty receptacle,"[9] ready to blindly receive someone else's knowledge and truth.

By problematizing the universal intellectual's "fixed truths," Judith Goleman, not unlike Foucault, calls our attention to the emergence of a "new kind of intellectual . . . along a new relationship of theory and practice." According to her, "the specific intellectual discovers that the complex forces—the conjunctures—that occur in particular settings, and constitute one's practice in its multiple effects, are themselves, what must be theorized as the dynamic 'truths' of that field. As such, a specific intellectual is, so to speak, an expert on these conjunctures, i.e., the multiple relations composing one's practice." For this reason, a teacher—as a specific intellectual—must question the received "truth" and its "unitary meaning" and reject the sectarianism of practitioners who are still not able to cut themselves free from the yoke of a colonialist legacy: "The colonist likes neither theory nor theorists. He who knows that he is in a bad ideological or ethical position generally boasts of being a man of action, one who draws his lesson from experience."[10]

Judith Goleman's *Working Theory* eloquently makes a convincing case against the function of the relationship between theory and practice so as to avoid the uncritical adoption of frozen methods that "undermine rather than support dialogic action," as exemplified by the pitfalls of the process approach to writing, to wit: "The way the sequenced writing assignments may actually contribute to a student's traditional role as the submissive subject of task work (the very kind of work that sequencing proponents have sought to avoid)." Practitioners' anti-theory postures often reduce the theoretical leading ideas to a fossilized dialogical method. I was reminded, for example, of some practitioners' unwillingness to engage Freire's leading ideas while readily adopting his methods by a sociolinguistics graduate student, who asked me why most professors in our graduate program talked about Freire's methods yet not a single professor required her to read any of Freire's books so as to study him.

For me, Judith Goleman's book, *Working Theory*, represents, par excellence, the ways in which practices are theorized so as to be critically understood. It also provides a sturdy intellectual base to support what I call an anti-method pedagogy that refuses the rigidity of models and methodological paradigms. In other words, an anti-method pedagogy points out the impossibility of dis-articulating methods from the theoretical principles that inform and shape them. By situating methods within a theoretical frame work that necessarily involves a power-relations analysis, educators cannot ignore their historical, racial, and privileged positions in the teaching and learning context. An anti-method pedagogy prevents the fragmentation of bodies of knowledge, methods versus theory, while it requires a critical understanding of the relationship among facts and their reason for existing. It necessarily involves critical reflection followed by political action. That is, to the extent that an anti-pedagogy demands a high degree of political clarity, it prevents the pseudocritical educator from romanticizing subordinate students and falling into a type of laissez-faire method of sharing experiences which, in the end, may result in a new form of paternalism. While an anti-method pedagogy would validate lived experiences, it would also require that we transcend experience so as to transform it into knowledge. Methods, divorced from the leading ideas that shape and maintain them, can never capture the complexity and contradiction inherent in a progressive and democratic pedagogy. Thus, a liberatory pedagogy should never be reduced to a method no matter how progressive it may appear.

The anti-method pedagogy calls to the educators' attention that it is not enough to find comfort in a method that pays lip service to anti-racism and social justice. It also reminds them of the enormous contradiction between their condemnation of oppression and their unwillingness to divest from their received "divine" privilege from the oppressive social orders. The anti-method pedagogy forces educators to transcend the "technicism" of methods and become transformative intellectuals who uphold "decent standards of behavior concerning freedom and justice from worldly powers or nations, and that deliberate or inadvertent violations of these standards need to be testified and fought against courageously."[11]

The anti-method pedagogy forces us to view the dialogical method as a form of social praxis so that sharing of experience is always informed by reflection and political action. Dialogue as social praxis "entails that recovering the voice of the oppressed is the fundamental condition for human emancipation."[12] By voice I do not mean a mere exchanging of experience as a form of group therapy, but rather a process that turns experience into critical reflection and political action. The anti-method pedagogy also frees us from the beaten path of certainties and specialism. It rejects the mechanization of intellectualism, and it prevents the bureaucratization of the mind. The anti-method pedagogy does not allow educators to accommodate a pedagogy of lies; it forces them to live in truth. No one could argue more pointedly against reducing dialogue and problem posing to a mere method than Freire:

> Problem posing education is revolutionary futurity. Hence, it is prophetic.... Hence it corresponds to the historical nature of man. Hence it affirms men as beings who transcend themselves.... Hence it identifies with the movement which engages men as being aware of their incompletion—an historical movement which has its point of departure, its subjects and its objective.[13]

The anti-method pedagogy not only adheres to Freire's view of education as revolutionary futurity, and Bakhtin's notion of "the ideological becoming of a human being," it also celebrates the eloquence of Antonio Machado's poem: "Caminante no hay camino, se hace el camino al andar."[14] Traveler, there is no road. The road is made as one walks.

—Donaldo Macedo

NOTES

1. A. W. France, *Composition as a Cultural Practice* (Westport, Conn: Bergin & Garvey, 1994), p. xviii.
2. W. E. Said, *Representations of the Intellectual* (New York: Pantheon Books, 1994), p. 15.
3. Ibid., pp. 4–5.
4. Ibid., p. 5.
5. Ibid. p. 9.
6. Ibid., p. 11.
7. Ibid.
8. P. Freire, *The Politics of Education* (South Hadley, Mass.: Bergin & Garvey, 1985), p. 116.
9. Ibid.
10. A. Memmi, *The Colonizer and the Colonized* (Boston: Beacon Press, 1991), p. 26.
11. W. E. Said, *Representations of the Intellectual* (New York: Pantheon Books, 1994), pp. 11–12.
12. S. Aronowitz, "Paulo Freire's Radical Democratic Humanism," in Peter McLaren and Peter Leonard (eds.), *Paulo Freire: A Critical Encounter* (London: Routledge, 1993), pp. 11–12.
13. P. Freire, *Pedagogy of the Oppressed* (New York: Continuum Publication Co., 1990), p. 72.
14. A. Manuel Machado, y Antonio Machado; *Obras Completas* (Madrid: Editorial Plenitud, 1962), p. 826.

Acknowledgments

I thank my editor and friend, Donaldo Macedo, for the invitation to contribute to his Series in Language and Ideology and for the generous support he has given me throughout this project. Because of the emphasis that composition studies places on postsecondary education, it has traditionally been separated from literacy studies whose emphasis has been on earlier stages of education. As a literacy scholar, Macedo has never subscribed to this distinction, believing instead that the relationship between language and ideology is a crucial point of departure for both composition and literacy scholars—if their work is to be critical. In the name of critical composition studies, Macedo invited me into his series, and for the opportunity to explore further our common ground, I am grateful.

I am also grateful to various members of the English Department at the University of Massachusetts–Boston whose work in the history of rhetoric, literacy, composition theory, and English as a second language has enriched my understanding and whose availability for spur-of-the-moment conversations has bolstered my confidence as I have been working on this project. These colleagues include John Brereton, Elinor Kutz, and Vivian Zamel. I direct special acknowledgment to my colleague emeritus, Ann Berthoff, whose fierce belief in the dialogic imagination has influenced me in ways I rediscover every day. As chair during the time that I was writing this book, Susan Horton did everything she could to create the right conditions for its completion, and for this, among other things, I thank her.

Rereading my manuscript in preparation for sending it to the publisher, I found myself imagining its reception by my colleagues from the University of Pittsburgh. My years as a graduate and postgraduate student at Pitt were formative, and I am grateful to the following people for their strong and enduring influence: William E. Coles, David Bartholomae, Mariolina Salvatori, Nick Coles, and Susan Wall.

Finally, I thank Neal Bruss, my husband and colleague, for his great help as a critical reader of my early drafts. His sense of parts and wholes allowed me to see the "book" as I wrote the chapters, editorially egging me past doubts. Not only did his comments help me to see the book that I was writing, but his fifty/fifty approach to child care helped me to organize my time into the kinds of chunks needed to make this perception possible.

When I began envisioning this project a number of years ago, I was oddly inspired by a retort made by Margaret Mead to something she had read by Harriet Beecher Stowe. In response to Stowe's complaint that she couldn't get any writing done because her baby cried so much, Mead said it wasn't because the baby cried so much, but because the baby *smiled* so much. Closer to my own expectations, Mead's reversal of common sense emboldened me to imagine one further reversal. As it turned out in my case—for many reasons—the baby's smiles, if anything, made writing *more* possible, and this is an acknowledgment I want to make as I send this book out to future writers.

ONE

Working Theory: Introduction

> *Interviewer:* You seem to have kept your distance from Marx and Marxism . . .
>
> *Foucault:* . . . I quote Marx without saying so. . . . When a physicist writes a work of physics, does he feel it necessary to quote Newton and Einstein?
>
> —Michel Foucault, *Power/Knowledge*, 52

Writing this introduction to *Working Theory* toward the end of the project, I am able to observe retrospectively how heavily I have been influenced by the works of Michel Foucault, often using them "without saying so." Unlike other theorists with whom I carry on direct dialogues in the chapters that follow, Foucault's analysis of power/knowledge/discourse relations informs these pages, orients the project, really, though without direct attribution. Rather than allowing his influence to remain tacit, I will try to articulate it here by way of introduction to the present volume. Indeed, even the title I have chosen cannot be understood in the way I intend it apart from a key concept of Foucault's—the concept of the specific intellectual and its difference from the universal intellectual. Thus, I will now turn to an elucidation of *Working Theory* in relation to Foucault's ideas about intellectuals.

In an interview with Foucault, published as "Truth and Power," Allesandro Fontana and Pasquale Pasquina ask the following question about the role of the intellectual in contemporary society:

> You have spoken previously of local struggles as the specific site of confrontation with power, outside and beyond all such global, general instances of parties or classes. What does this imply about the role of intellectuals? If one . . . doesn't purport to function as the bringer, the master of truth, what position is the intellectual to assume? (Foucault, 1980: 126–27)

Foucault's answer to this question, as it involves a description of the specific intellectual, is relevant to the field of composition and its debate over the traditional role of the writing instructor as the master reader of students' truth-statements. This masterly role can no longer be taken for granted in composition any more than in society at large, and those who have questioned it have often done so with reference to Foucault. By reconnecting the traditionally transcendent values of knowledge and truth to worldly networks of power relations that are materialized in discourse, Foucault, by implication, puts traditional approaches to composition (and its assumptions about knowledge) under radical review. In recent years, many composition scholars have taken up such a review. For instance, in *Fragments of Rationality* (1992), Lester Faigley looks at the way traditional assumptions about truth and knowledge have led to the valorization of the confessional narrative in modern composition studies and to the privileged role of the receiver of these confessions—the teacher:

> Those teachers of writing who define good writing as truth-telling assume that truth comes from within and can be conveyed transparently through language. The teacher as receiver of truth takes the position of bearer of authority who can certify truth. . . . The authority to determine which truths are universal places the teacher in a position of privilege because the teacher is outside of the petty interests of history but within the boundaries of universal truth. Such an assignment of authority through a teacher's claim to recognize truth is characteristic of Foucault's description of the modern exercise of power. (131)

On the basis of this connection between truth and power, Faigley (131) questions the traditional role of the writing teacher as the master reader of universal values, asking instead, "[W]hat power relations come into play when [teachers] give a writing assignment that encourages students to make revealing personal disclosures?" Because this masterful role is challenged in various contexts, it seems that similarly fundamental questions about how to proceed follow. For instance, as Fontana and Pasquina ask, "What position is the intellectual to assume?" so too in the particular context of composition, Kurt Spellmeyer (1993:71) asks, "[W]hat should writing teachers teach?" One purpose of this introduction is to suggest that an answer to the second question—What should writing teachers teach?—depends, in part, on how we answer the first question—What position is the intellectual to assume?

Responding to this first question, Foucault compares the role of specific intellectuals with the role of universal intellectuals. Universal intellectuals (whose day has passed, he believes) work in the modality of the "exemplary," "the just-and-true-for-all," whereas specific intellectuals work "within specific sectors at the precise points where their own conditions of life or work situate them" (1980:136). Where universal intellectuals derive from the figure of the jurist, specific intellectuals derive from the expert. As examples of the latter, Foucault points to Charles Darwin and J. Robert Oppenheimer, biologist and physicist, respectively, who, on the basis of their expertise, began "to intervene in contemporary struggles in the name of a 'local' scientific truth—however important the latter may be" (129). (Foucault subsequently qualifies his choice of Darwin, saying it is actually "the post-Darwinian evolutionists" who faced the extension of technical and scientific matters into the economic and social domain, re-forming them as specific intellectuals [129].) In any case, Foucault maintains that it is precisely the *conjunctural* nature of these intellectuals' work that makes it so different from the unified work of the master intellectual. In regard to Oppenheimer, Foucault writes that as a result of Oppenheimer's precise scientific knowledge and institutional status, "for the first time . . . the intellectual was hounded by political powers, no longer on account of a general discourse which he conducted, but because of the knowledge at his disposal" (128).

At this conjuncture of political struggle and local scientific truth, a new kind of intellectual emerges, along with a new relationship between theory and practice (126). Where the universal intellectual applies fixed truths to particular settings (Foucault cites Zola's naturalism as a case in point), the specific intellectual discovers that the complex of forces—the conjunctures—that occur in particular settings, and constitute one's practice in its multiple effects, are themselves what must be theorized as the dynamic "truths" of that field. As such, a specific intellectual is, so to speak, an expert on these conjunctures, that is, the multiple relations composing one's practice. Working these relations for the knowledge they will yield on many levels, specific intellectuals eschew universal theory for a theory of the contextual; in place of unitary meaning, they substitute disseminated effects. The risk for one working as a theorist of these specific conjunctural effects, as Foucault sees it, is that of becoming too specific and thus isolated by this work. However, this risk can be reduced by defining the work of the specific intellectual in ways that do not lead one into overspecialization and loss of contact with others. Defining the work of the specific intellectual as "three-fold," Foucault tries to mix the local with the general. Not only is the specific intellectual defined by his or her "class position" and "conditions of life and work" as an intellectual, but also by the way the "politics of truth" impinge on that work:

> And it's with this last factor that his position can take on a general significance and that his local, specific struggle can have effects and implications which are not simply professional or sectoral. The intellectual can operate and struggle at the general level of that regime of truth which is so essential to the structure and functioning of our society. (132)

In the end, Foucault seems to be suggesting that specific intellectuals need to understand the precise conjuncture of technical, political, and economic forces in their particular spheres of work, *not* in order to cleanse them of ideological impurities, but in order to contribute to an understanding of how these spheres of work are reproducing an unequal regime through their specific forms of knowledge and truth. "[I]t's not a matter of a battle 'on behalf' of the truth," Foucault writes, "but of a battle about the status of truth and the economic and political role it plays" (132). By understanding the current "politics of truth" in our particular fields, specific intellectuals are in better positions to change those politics,

Working Theory 5

to detach "the power of truth from the forms of hegemony, social, economic and cultural, within which it operates at the present time" (133).

Working the theories of knowledge and systems of truth that are working them, specific intellectuals in effect redefine knowledge and truth as worldly things and, in so doing, begin to alter the systems of statements and procedures that have produced these concepts. As the subtitle of this book is meant to suggest, working theory in the manner of Foucault's specific intellectuals is an appropriate action for both teachers and students of composition. Anything less would collapse the teacher's role back into the role of the universal intellectual—one, for example, who advises students on "the regime of truth," its systems, procedures, and effects. Such an error in educational relations, which is all too common, is a result of completely misunderstanding that teachers who seek to change the consciousness of their students are reproducing the very "regime of truth" they would criticize. Only when the actual work of students and teachers is commonly—if differently—directed toward a specific understanding of the systems of knowledge and truth they are both in and the effects these systems produce could one say that the tide of specific inquiry is lifting all boats.

So far, I have only hinted at the relevance of these issues and concepts for composition, and I could not fault a reader for finding the above rather far afield. Indeed, what follows in chapters 2 through 5 does not hold out the promise of a systematic answer to the question, "What should writing teachers teach?" Rather, what follows could be said to be the various ways I have rediscovered this question itself and why it needs to be asked. As the directions from which I approach this question differ from chapter to chapter, so, too, do the responses. In every case, however, a critique of knowledge as transcendent and the intellectual as universal motivates the question and the search for alternative procedures in the specific context of composition.

Composition—whose traditional function has been to codify the reigning ideas of knowledge and truth through its lessons on how to write—could not, it would seem, be a more relevant point of focus for this kind of inquiry. For not only have intellectuals in composition reproduced these traditional values in their textbooks and classroom methods, but they have also adapted them to the political struggles of the day in which they are immersed. For instance, despite their historical embracing of the great writer as the figure of the universal intellectual par excellence (thus concurring with Foucault), traditional composition educators themselves never aimed, in their materials, to foster great, or even very good, writers—only relatively correct ones. A specific intellectual working in composition would have to ask why such a gap has existed between the high value placed on "writers" and the low value placed on students who write.

Indeed, only the teaching of fiction, poetry, and drama has retained the word "writing" in its categorization as "creative writing." Everything else is "composition"—that is, "not Writing." This history and these politics of composition are not separable from the pedagogical decisions that have been taken in its name. Thus, an expert in composition needs to understand the precise conjunctures of technical, political, and economic forces working composition to certain effects. It is my argument as well that students who arrive for composition instruction should learn—as the very enactment of what we mean by reading and writing—to share in this inquiry. Students who would learn from us "how to write" would learn that we cannot offer them technical procedures or interesting processes alone, but in conjunction with the worldviews, subject positions, and regimes of truth that they are part of. Working the theories that are working them as students of composition, they would join their teachers in redefining what intellectual inquiry involves and why.

Each chapter in this book pursues the question of what this intellectual inquiry involves and why—for teachers, for students, and for the relationship between them. In Chapter 2, I borrow from the works of Louis Althusser to ask the fundamental question alluded to above: What is it to read? Pursuing this question gives me an opportunity to discuss the differences between idealist and materialist epistemologies as Althusser construes them from his reading of Marx. Broadly speaking, the differences between these two epistemologies parallel the differences between the universal and specific intellectual developed by Foucault. Thus, by defining Althusser's materialist epistemology, which he calls structural causality, I have begun to articulate a theory of knowledge for the specific intellectual as well.

A large part of Chapter 2 focuses on drawing out the pedagogical implications of this epistemology. For the student of composition, I offer a theory of agency—critical effectivity—that correlates with this epistemology. The concept of critical effectivity presupposes that a knowledge of writing in relation to the worldviews, subject positions, and regimes of truth it is part of cannot be learned all at once or once and for all. Rather, this knowledge is specific in its effects and thus must be learned over and over in its effects. What such learning looks like and what it accomplishes for college writers are two issues developed here.

In Chapter 3, I work with the theory of language developed by Mikhail Bakhtin in order to explore the effects of authoritative language relations on students' reading and writing practices. If Chapter 2 defines and illustrates what it can mean to read and write in the manner of a specific intellectual, Chapter 3 defines the authoritative forces opposing such practices in students' own discourse relations. In this chapter, the universal intellectual is not someone "out there" dispensing truth, but a rigid, authoritarian voice composing a student's discourse with herself and others. It is Bakhtin's thesis that the array of discourses composing one's subjectivity must be reviewed and interanimated, that is, put into dialogue with one another, in order for critical consciousness to emerge.

This ongoing process of dialogic review resembles the work of the specific intellectual who must work the theories that are working her, who must be an expert on the conjunctural effects of the various competing discourses constructing one's relations to work and school, self and society. As these capacities for dialogic interanimation develop, what Bakhtin calls internally persuasive language relations begin to develop too. These internally persuasive relations do not represent the "finding of one's own voice," but rather the finding of a method for understanding and acting on the conjunctural effects of one's many voices. In addition to associating such dialogical thinking with the reading and writing practices of specific intellectuals, Chapter 3 uses a case study method to consider the ongoing, antidialogical effects of authoritative discourse relations on the writing of one student.

As Chapter 3 does, so, too, Chapter 4 concerns itself with the ambiguities that may attend students' activations of dialogue with the academic discourses they have learned and are learning. Reviewing the scholarly debate about such work, I give qualified support to the position that students of composition should study the conjunctural effects of the academic genres they would learn, including the freshman English essay. As students learn to read the forms their schooling takes, the way these forms shape their knowledge and their notions of truth to certain purposes, a distancing effect begins to occur which has been described honorifically in the literature as critical nonidentification with one's subject positions and discourses (Aronowitz and Giroux, 1991: 120) This critical stance resembles a relationship to knowledge that Bakhtin calls "relativized consciousness" (324). However, through my review of the writing of a particularly able student in the midst of such work, it is possible to see how difficult it can be to distinguish critical nonidentification from premature *dis*-identification with subject positions deemed out of favor. Teachers who choose to work with their students toward some distance and perspective on academic writing procedures, in the manner of specific intellectuals, should expect the residual effects of traditional master/student relations to color the results of such work in ways that may even threaten the credibility of the whole project.

Indeed, in the final chapter I address a key essay of Stanley Fish in which he *does* denounce the credibility of such a project. In his essay, "Anti-foundationalism, Theory Hope and the Teaching of Composition," Fish (1989) argues that to invite students into a working relationship with their situations as writers is to invite them into a review of what is ongoing and therefore *impossible* of review. My response includes reference to the concept of critical effectivity developed in Chapter 2, a concept that assumes criticity itself as partial and ongoing. Moreover, I use the Fish essay as an opportunity to review the exclusionary uses to which literacy has been put in secondary and postsecondary education so as to ask how we can possibly accept Fish's call for a return to the "basics," given the prejudicial and disciplinary uses of these "basics" throughout the history of American education.

Over and above this response to Fish, I try to address his criticism of teachers who would apply a situational theory of knowledge to their pedagogical practice in a manner that fixes it as a new form of universal knowledge. I suggest that this contradiction can be greatly avoided if students research their own relations to their discourses, thereby developing materials by which teachers may learn about their students' situations. When teachers work with student writing in this way, they are using it to continue their own becoming as specific intellectuals; they are not using it to apply universals about situationality onto passive students and their intransitive texts. Working the specific language relations that are working them, students educate their teachers regarding their limits and possibilities for dialogic becoming. Actually historical, these dynamic student–teacher relations are also actively rhetorical. The teacher is not a master of situation, but a student of it. Indeed, by accepting and working with situation, history, politics, and convention dynamically, such teachers and students, I would argue, challenge the current regime of truth and its claims of universal knowledge without obstructing anyone's access to this situation, these conventions—as I hope the student writing that I work with here will show.

TWO

Reading and Writing: Working the Dialectic since Marx

> However paradoxical it may seem, I venture to suggest that our age threatens one day to appear in the history of human culture as marked by the most dramatic and difficult trial of all, the discovery of and training in the meaning of the "simplest" acts of existence: seeing, listening, speaking, reading . . . only since Freud have we begun to suspect what listening, and hence what speaking (and keeping silent), *means*; that this *"meaning"* of speaking and listening reveals beneath the innocence of speech and hearing the culpable depth of a second, *quite different* discourse, the discourse of the unconscious. I dare maintain that only since Marx have we begun to suspect what, in theory at least, *reading* and hence writing *means*.
> —Louis Althusser, *Reading Capital*

I

In his essay "From *Capital* to Marx's Philosophy," Louis Althusser interprets Marx's masterwork from the point of view of neither an economist nor an historian, but a philosopher. He attempts to theorize the way of reading that Marx practiced in *Capital* but did not conceptualize. By asking the question that he believes underpins Marx's process—"What is it to read?"—Althusser disturbs our assumptions regarding the obvious, taken-for-granted nature of reading. In the way that the question, "What is it to read?" problematizes our habits of literacy, its asking could be said to enact the "way of reading" which Althusser proceeds to theorize in Marx.

For those of us who would teach reading and writing, it is of no little importance that these activities are also concepts, and, as such, have meanings that change. As the privileged status of current scholarship that considers reading and writing as interpretive activities would attest, the present meaning of reading and writing *has* been changing from that of a simple, text-centered, linear process to a complex and reflexive act of mind in society. Seeing ourselves seeing, reading ourselves reading—these are the codifications of the "discovery" of those " 'simplest' acts of existence" to which Althusser alludes. For teachers and students alike, a discovery of their complexity has certainly constituted a "difficult trial": the trial of learning to think about the sources of our thought conscientiously and problematically, that is to say, dialectically.

It would be a misrepresentation of Althusser, however, to read the opening passage only in terms that translate Marx's particular discovery of the dialectic into a call for the cultivation of self-consciousness and a pluralistic perspective. Since Marx, what reading and writing *can* mean is more specific than this. For what it can mean goes beyond knowing *that* we interpret when we read and write to *how* these interpretations themselves are part of a dialogue in the play of social history whose theater is the world. It is a play, which, for the most part, our students perform in a house darkened and silenced by the bright lights and din of their worldliness. Restoring the dialogue and seeing the play that we are in constitutes a Marxian perspective which, in truth, is not so much a perspective in itself as a means for getting behind our perspectives and analyzing their social and historical functions as knowledge.

Only since Marx, Althusser argues, have we come to suspect that reading and writing—as concepts and as functions—are historically determined and, hence, determining constructions of knowledge. They are not natural or timeless acts through which meaning flows; rather, they are historically contingent acts that compose the meaning we make. As Althusser asserts above, only since Marx have we come to look at these traditionally timeless, neutral, "simple" acts of existence as not timeless but historically contingent, as not neutral but value-laden, as not simple but complex. By turning reading and writing into historical problems themselves, Marx can be said to have discovered a new way of reading and writing which constitutes a new theory of history as well. Thus, it is to the *reading* of history as conceptualized by Althusser that we must turn in order to discover what "in theory at least" reading and writing mean since Marx.

Let us begin with what Althusser thinks the concepts of reading and hence writing do not mean since Marx: they do not mean the "immediate reading of essence in existence" on the religious model of Hegel's Absolute Knowledge (*Reading*, 9); and they do not mean the abstraction of the essential from the inessential on the empiricist model (37). Because both of these models require that we read knowledge as a real part of a real object, they are, for the purposes of understanding Marx's difference, more alike as idealisms than not (38).

These idealist conceptions of a reality that contains an immediate and discoverable essence—as a nut in a shell or a meaning in a story—imply an epistemology that separates and abstracts a real essence from a real object. Marx's work represents a challenge to these theories of knowledge. In his study of political economy, Marx poses questions that had never been asked before because a theory of knowledge as essence, by its very nature, blocks knowledge from being thought of as a concept, as a *theory*. A belief in knowledge as an essence forecloses an investigation of knowledge as a human production, and it was ultimately Marx's breakthrough to question the historical function of this belief itself. To look at an ahistorical teleology as an historical production constitutes what Althusser has called Marx's "epistemological break" (*For Marx*, 33). As Althusser suggests below, this break, if we are to understand it, obligates us to reconstruct our own thinking:

> We are thereby obliged to renounce every teleology of reason, and to conceive the historical relation between a result and its condition of existence as a relation of production, and not of expression, and therefore as what, in a phrase that clashes with the classical system of categories and demands the *replacement* of those categories themselves, we can call the *necessity of its contingency*. To grasp this necessity we must grasp the very special and paradoxical logic of the conditions of the production of knowledge. (*Reading*, 45)

Once we have grasped the notion that knowledge itself is a human production, we are forever after on different terrain. Knowledge of an object seen as an act of conceptualization is a type of knowledge that cannot be said to be identical with the object itself. Only by analyzing the specific social and historic logic of the form our knowledge takes—its "contingency"—can we derive insight into the object of knowledge itself.

To argue that an artifact or text is present for us only as an object of our knowledge is not, however, to fall into an "idealism of consciousness" or subjectivity, for these thought processes called consciousness are themselves effects of structure. In the following statement, Althusser's insistence on the historicity of consciousness and thought can be observed:

> Far from being an essence opposed to the material world, the faculty of a "pure" transcendental subject or "absolute consciousness", i.e., the myth that idealism produces as a myth in which to recognize and establish itself, "thought" is a peculiar real system, established on and articulated to the real world of a given historical society . . . defined by the conditions of . . . a *peculiar structure.* (*Reading*, 42)

All knowledge, even the knowledge of how we produce knowledge, must be understood historically as the particular effects of social structure. The concept of a "transcendental subject" or "absolute consciousness" represents a certain type of individual for a certain reading, an absolute or idealist reading.

The theory of knowledge that Althusser names as structural causality, on the other hand, does not require a transcendental subject for attributing meaning. Structural causality is based on the principle that all knowledge must be understood historically as the particular effects of a social structure. As a philosopher, Althusser assigned himself the task of theorizing the practice that Marx himself did not name "because the age Marx lived in did not provide him, and he could not acquire in his lifetime an adequate concept with which to think what he produced: *the concept of the effectivity of a structure on its elements*" (*Reading*, 29). Structural effectivity (or causality) represents, for Althusser, a radical break with idealist (or expressive) causality:

The Dialectic since Marx

> [Structural causality] can be entirely summed up in the concept of *"Darstellung"* the key epistemological concept of the whole Marxist theory of value, the concept whose object is precisely to designate the mode of *presence* of the structure in its *effects*.... The structure is not an essence *outside* the economic phenomena which comes and alters their aspect, forms and relations ... on the contrary ... the structure is immanent in its effects, is nothing outside its effects. (*Reading*, 188–89)

In this statement, Althusser argues that the mode of production constitutes the entire system of social relations. A mode of production (traditionally designated as the economic base) is actually everywhere as the whole system of social relationships and nowhere as a metaphysical or empirical presence. (Althusser does retain the notion of economic determination "in the last instance," but qualifies this by adding that the "lonely hour of the last instance never comes" [*For Marx*, 111, 113]).

Once we have come to think of knowledge as a structural effect, it is possible to see that a thinking person does not uncover knowledge as if it were hidden in an artifact or text, but as something the thinking person has construed, based on the combined histories of seer and seen. What one sees and does not see is not so much an effect of individual wisdom or ignorance as it is an effect of a larger field of beliefs and assumptions defining the visible and invisible to a purpose. Althusser calls this the "field of the problematic" which constitutes "the forms in which all problems must be posed at any given moment" (*Reading*, 25). Extrapolating from Marx's reading of classical political economy, Althusser observes that in any field of inquiry, the researcher and the discipline are necessarily related by the theoretical assumptions that structure the field of possibility for both. What a person does not see or does not question is defined by the field of the problematic as much as what a person does see and does question. Oversight is a form of sight; nonvision, a form of vision. From this insight, Althusser develops a theory of reading in which he understands such relations not as binary opposites or as absolutes, but as relations necessary to the terrain of a particular structure. It is finally, he asserts, Marx's distinction to have seen this terrain *as* a terrain, that is, as a structure and not an eternal form.

When we know a structure through essences, we are prevented from asking questions about it which we can ask when we know a structure through our inferred logic of its productions. This explains why Marx wrote of Hegel and the Young Hegelians: "not only in their answers but in their questions there was a mystification" (*For Marx*, 80). This also explains why Marx's theories constitute a break from Hegel's dialectic, not a reversal, not a turning of Hegel on his feet again. "A man on his head is the same man when he is finally walking on his feet," Althusser has written, and Marx's interrogation of the terrain itself, the field of the problematic that structures meaning, places him on new terrain and within a different problematic—not on Hegel's terrain or in his shoes (73).

It is important to pursue the differences between the Hegelian and Marxian dialectic further because the differences have implications for our subject: what reading and writing mean since Marx. In *Marxism and Form* (1974), Fredric Jameson takes the position that both the Hegelian and Marxian dialectics are forms of self-consciousness with the Hegelian dialectic raising our awareness of the way thought processes themselves limit thought, and the Marxian dialectic raising our awareness of the political and historical nature of that thought (340). Hegel, Jameson argues, understood the contradiction inherent in the effort to analyze the thought that limits thought while one remains inside those limits. Hegel's "notion of the Absolute Idea, of that 'Sunday of Life' when history stops," Jameson writes, "is clearly the ultimate working out of the contradiction" (364). Marx's rejection of this transcendent place of reflection results in a fully historicized theory of knowing by which to define the problem of history itself dialectically. Jameson writes:

> As soon . . . as one is able to feel one's own thought as a historical action on equal terms with the objects studied . . . then the Hegelian contradiction is overcome, and one no longer has to posit an end to history in order for historical thought to take place. In the apprehension of all events, mental or otherwise, as profoundly historical and situational in character, Marx's thought represents an advance over that of Hegel, who reserved a single position outside of history for the philosopher of history himself, and was to that extent

unable to grasp the notion of being-in-situation in its most paradoxical dimensions. (364–65)

This "being-in-situation" which may appear only to constitute another relativism is, however, no such thing. The Marxian dialectic does not constitute a numbing skepticism. Rather, the Marxian dialectic constitutes a hermeneutic method by which to account historically for the critical limitations of such a response as skepticism. What, we must ask, are the social and historical conditions that have produced this concept as a solution, and what are the conditions that have produced the forms of the problems that "gave rise" to it as well (Jameson, 1974: 373)?

By virtue of these questions, then, the Marxian dialectic is not so much a system in itself as a response to a system, a means by which to analyze the dominant social and historical forces producing structures of meaning. Let us call this hermeneutic method, ideological analysis, where by *ideology* we mean a particular practice of "representation" (Althusser, 1971: 162). In capitalist society—the object of Marx's study—the practice of representation is dominated by the class that dominates the forces of production and struggles to maintain that position. And so, while ideology, as the practice of representation, may be an organic part of every social structure, it does not function in the same way in every structure. In a structure determined by its contradictory relations of power and privilege, ideology can be "seen" as the representation of these contradictions as normal, as human nature itself.

As the practice of representation and the construction of individuals as subjects for those representations, ideology is a material force that naturalizes the unequal relations of production—the ongoing, complex, multiply determined interrelations among classes, races, genders, ages, disciplines, and more (Althusser, 1971: 170). By virtue of its naturalizing effects, ideology limits individuals to a certain "mental horizon" (Coward and Ellis, 1977: 74). The pedagogical function of historical materialism, then, is that it can teach us to "see" ideology in our representations; it can teach us to "read" ideology as a specific organization of reality and therefore to create the possibility of changing that reality. Reading the world ideologically means that we look at the social structure as a structuring; it means that we trace the course from contradictory social relations to their naturalization. This state of contradiction, however, as Althusser has written, is "never simple but specified by the historically concrete forms and circumstances in which it is exercised." In other words, "the apparently simple [Capital-Labor] contradiction is always overdetermined" (*For Marx*, 106). Because all contradictions are historically concrete and multiply or overdetermined, ideology cannot exist as a thing in itself; rather, it exists only in its own specific effects as the practice of representation. Consequently, ideological analysis is a responsive hermeneutic—even a "negative hermeneutic"—by which we can reconstruct (or deconstruct) the naturalized forms of contradiction where we read them (Jameson, 1981: 286).

Extending the argument that ideology exists only in its effects, we arrive at the insight that critical understanding and the capacity for resistance to ideology similarly can exist only in their effects: there is no criticity or resistance to ideology's effects once and for all. The historicizing concept of overdetermined contradiction prevents this. Thus, critical individuals are dialecticians—continually re-seeing their subjectivity and acting on what they see as it evolves and is transformed by circumstance. With this in mind, it could be said that Althusser's discovery of structural effectivity implies a material theory of human agency that can be named critical effectivity. The concept of critical effectivity presupposes that knowledge of one's subjectivity cannot be learned in the fixed or static manner of a "history lesson" but rather must be understood over and over again in its effects. As such, critical effectivity also defines a method of interpretation and a pedagogical practice that will be explored in the third section of this chapter.

As the form of agency implied by structural effectivity (Althusser's "key epistemological concept"), critical effectivity is worth pursuing further, especially because Althusser has been criticized as lacking a theory of agency, a theory of how and why people may resist a structure's dominating effects. Those who criticize Althusser for his determinism typically focus on his essay, "Ideology and Ideological State Apparatuses." It is possible, however, to find in that essay some continuity with theories of structural effectivity—despite its deterministic thrust. For the most part, this continuity can be found in Althusser's emphasis on the material quality of ideology and thus (by implication) the material (versus essential) quality of its critique.

The essay's deterministic thrust is evident in Althusser's schematic presentation of ideological institutions as sites for reproducing individuals who will passively participate in the dominant forms of production (*Lenin*, 154). Naming the educational ideological state apparatus (ISA) as the most important one (152), Althusser attributes to it the capacity to provide each individual "the role it has to fulfill in class society: the role of the exploited . . . the role of the agent of exploitation . . . of the agent of repression . . . or the professional ideologist" (156).

An important criticism of Althusser's analysis of the school's determining effects comes from Henry Giroux in *Theory and Resistance in Education* (1978). Noting the determinism in Althusser's representation of education, Giroux complains that his analysis leaves no room for struggle or opposition within school walls: "This is no small point," he writes, "because it suggests that schools are *not* to be viewed as social sites marked by the interplay of domination, accommodation, and struggle, but rather as sites that function smoothly to reproduce a docile labor force" (82). Although it is not hard to see how such a criticism can be made of Althusser's analysis of the educational ISA, it does ignore other statements in the essay regarding struggle and resistance in the various apparatuses. For instance, Althusser writes that the "ISAs may be not only the *stake*, but the *site* of class struggle, and often of bitter forms of class struggle" (147). There are, he goes on to explain, more opportunities for the expression of resistance in ideological structures than in largely repressive structures, because, in part, the contradictory nature of the ideological apparatus is more able to be turned against itself (147).

Over and above these specific references to resistance in the ISAs, it is important to note that Althusser concedes the sketchy, even rudimentary, nature of his essay and the need for further working out its implications. His discussion of the ISAs, he writes, "will obviously have to be examined in detail, tested, corrected and reorganized" (143). What is not so obvious is the nature of the corrections to be made. However, if one looks closely at the themes of Althusser's earlier writings and their implications for the question, "What is it to read?" it would seem necessary to examine and correct the idealist tendencies of the ISA essay. Further attention needs to be given to the apparent inconsistency between Althusser's key concept of structural effectivity and the totalizing approach he tends to take toward education. As Giroux has argued, Althusser seems to be looking at education's appearance of totality in a way that precludes an analysis by its participants of its historicity. However, following Althusser's theory of structural effectivity, we may see that the educational apparatus (which exists in its effects) can logically only impose itself in its effects.

Effectivity, as a theory, deprives any structure or apparatus the privilege of being empowered as a seamless whole. Certainly, the intensity of educational practices and rituals, especially as this affects children, produces the appearance of totality, but the practice of structural effectivity is intended to allow us to historicize and demystify this appearance. Regardless of the ideological "density" of an apparatus, its materiality as a structure in its effects implies its knowability *as* a structure in its effects. To be sure, the knowledge will be partial, itself subject to the laws of contradiction and overdetermination. However, our impatience with the fact of situated knowledge cannot be used to fault it, except within an idealist problematic based on essential knowledge.

In a later section of his ISA essay, Althusser would appear to confirm this conclusion by virtue of the method he describes for ideological recognition within a material framework. In that section, Althusser discusses the need for "our incessant practice of ideological recognition" along with "*knowledge* of the mechanism of this recognition" (173). Incessant recognition of ideology's effects and mechanisms could be said to define critical effectivity in the way that it replaces conclusive knowledge of an object's ideological essence with a process of continuous historicizing of an object in an overdetermined and contradictory setting. There is nothing in this definition of critical effectivity that would exclude education from its terms. Indeed, one could say that rather than being beyond ideological investigation—as Althusser seems to argue—education is particularly well suited to such an "incessant practice," given its daily structure.

In his essay, Althusser found the struggle for critical knowledge within the educational apparatus to be hopelessly trivial and ultimately reproductive of the dominant system. But the very nature of effectivity (as defined by Althusser) is its partial, incremental quality. It is unclear how such incremental or partial recognition of ideology's form and content could be condemned as trivial or merely reproductive *except* against a theory of total recognition (against which we have seen Althusser argue). Thus, one could conclude that Althusser worked out his theory of structural causality more clearly in terms of production than reproduction and that it is for current readers to make appropriate corrections.

Two purposes for critical work in education are working with students to read the forms of their (and our) individuality and learning together the mechanisms of this reading. These purposes cannot be negated by the fact that education will always also involve reproduction of contradictory social relations. Nowhere else does Althusser presuppose the absence of contradiction for the performance of ideological recognition. Indeed, the process of ideological recognition, by its nature, *is* performed in the midst of contradiction. Not only does critical effectivity describe a method fitted to the structure of daily classroom work, but it also describes a new type of critical subject—not a "converted" subject, critical once and for all, but a critical subject in his or her effects, uneven as that may be.

To conclude this section, we could say that a pedagogy of knowing based on revised Althusserian principles makes possible a new way of reading and writing—a way in which one reads texts closely as part of a social process in contradiction. This would include one's own critical reading practices and the writing that emerges from them. All writing thus becomes rewriting in that it entails re-presenting a cultural artifact's form in terms of the specific social dialogue it is part of. Seeing the not-seen, hearing the not-heard, constitutes the Marxian dialectic as an act of dialogical restoration, one that cannot be accomplished without an understanding of the historical problematic that has structured (and to a certain extent continues to structure) these visions as nonvisions, these voices as silences. Using the concept of hegemony developed by Antonio Gramsci to denote the lived experience of cultural contradiction, Jameson writes: "the stress on the dialogical . . . allows us to reread or rewrite the hegemonic forms themselves" (1981: 86). This, then, could be said to be, if not a stopping point, at least a point of provisional closure for the student writer engaged by the perpetual motion machine of the Marxian hermeneutic. When a dialogue is restored; when hegemonic relations are perceived; when a form is understood ideologically as a specific way of seeing, reading, and representing the world—when the student of the Marxian dialectic has done all this—he or she has begun to practice a new discourse and can be said to be a participant in "the most dramatic and difficult trial of all, the discovery of and training in the meaning of the 'simplest' acts of existence: seeing, listening, speaking, reading" and hence writing.

II

It is, of course, one thing to propose these goals of critical effectivity for students of the historical materialist dialectic, and another to design semester-long courses that are means toward those goals. Put another way, it is one thing to teach the current model of composing as a formal, dialectical process and another to teach that meaning itself is dialectical and historical. In *Textual Carnivals: The Politics of Composition* (1991), Susan Miller presents reasons for the current dominance of the process model in composition studies as well as a critique of its dominance. The process-centered model and its counterpart, the product-centered model, broadly characterize the two schools of thought in recent American composition studies. In her definitive essay, "The Winds of Change: Thomas Kuhn and the Revolution in the Teaching of Writing" (1982), Maxine Hairston characterizes the product-centered model by its emphasis on the finished written product, especially its conformity to the classical modes of rhetoric: description, narration, exposition, and argument. "Its adherents," she writes, "believe that competent writers know what they are going to say before they begin to write; thus their most important task when they are preparing to write is finding a form into which to organize content." This task, she continues, is seen as essentially linear, proceeding from prewriting to writing to rewriting (78).

In contrast, adherents of the process-centered model focus on invention and assume that writers discover what they want to say as they write. Rather than linear, writing is viewed as a recursive, dialectical process, without clear-cut stages (86). "Writers write, plan, revise, anticipate and review throughout the writing process ... without any apparent plan," says Hairston, who is herself an advocate of this model: "They develop their topics intuitively, not methodically" (85). Thus, she argues, composition research and pedagogy should focus on an understanding of these intuitive mechanisms and the way they can be fostered for individual growth in writing.

Working with these features of the product and process models, Miller observes that, for all their differences, both models derive from a common Western tradition, one in which the individual as writer " 'originates,' 'generates,' and 'conceives' discourse" (113). Along with this concept of individuality, Miller argues that both models assume that "meanings reside 'behind' a text in essentialized 'minds' and that there are secrets to 'grasping' them" (114). The progressive reputation attaching to current process models may thus be more apparent than real, for, finally, process-centered research and pedagogy have a largely dehistoricizing and isolating function, encouraging students to engage in the writing process "for-its-own-sake" (94). In this way, the function of the process model of composition (broadly speaking) has been similar to the function of the New Criticism in literary studies. Both put forward an "almost entirely formalist and intransitive vision of writing," one that isolates students and depoliticizes the values being fostered (97). These values, as identified by Terry Eagleton in "The Subject of Literature," include sensitivity, creativity, perceptiveness, and reflectiveness. For the subject of the process model as well as the subject of New Criticism, the goal is the same: a person who, in Eagleton's words, "is sensitive, receptive, imaginative and so on ... *about nothing in particular*" (quoted in Miller, 1991: 91). From this point of view, it is arguable that the process model—especially its expressive and cognitive forms—has been at the expense of a more historical and critical study of writing and meaning. Instruction in the formal dialectic of composing has substituted for instruction in the social dialectic of interpretation, which elsewhere has been re-reforming disciplines.

As Miller observes, however, the struggle within composition studies has not been simply bipolar, between product and process advocates only. Within the process model itself, various tendencies have developed, some more socially disposed than others (see Berlin, 1988; Faigley, 1986; Knoblauch, 1988). A good example of a composition theorist trying to bridge the gap between the formal and social dialectics of composing is Ann Berthoff. In the 1980s, Berthoff's thought about the making of meaning (her signature concept) was influenced by the work of the radical Brazilian educator, Paulo Freire. Especially important was his emphasis on problem-posing education whereby "significant dimensions of an individual's contextual reality" are named and analyzed in the process of learning to read and write (Freire, 1968: 95). This critical process of *conscientization* by which men and women discover themselves to be "in a situation" deepens their historical awareness and capacity for investigative uses of their literacy. "He differentiates *decoding*—matching sound and letter shape—from *decodification*, which is interpretation," Berthoff wrote in 1986, "in order to assure that they not be pedagogically separated" (125–26). In her effort to apply this connection to North American classrooms, Berthoff argued that students must be given opportunities to "look and look again . . . at texts and the topography of their own lives" (127). Referring to her dialectical method of composing by which students learn a process for looking and looking again, she continued, "Writing dialectically encourages, as it *requires*, conscientization, the critical consciousness of oneself as meaning-maker" (128).

This is certainly true in the sense that writers who are put in the process wherein they may watch themselves figuring something are in the position to watch themselves as figurers, discovering the constitutive power of their own perspectives, and by extension, the constitutive power of perspectives beyond their own. In short, the dialectic of composing introduces writers to the historical contingency of meaning, to meaning as dependent on particular contexts and perspectives. Without a doubt, this "encourages as it *requires*" new critical consciousness regarding the old idealism of fixed meaning, that is, of meaning as an essence that resides in its object. Writers who learn through their own composing processes that meaning is situational, which is to say, a matter of specific contexts and perspectives, are writers who are coming into consciousness of history itself, and indeed, of the complex constitutive relations among history, self, and knowledge.

At this threshold of dialectical self-consciousness, however, where one is both thinking about an object and observing oneself thinking about it, differences emerge in the forms that the self-consciousness may take. These differences between forms of awareness about one's writing practice broadly distinguish the Hegelian from the Marxian dialectic as Jameson describes it:

> For Hegel . . . the thinker comes to understand the way in which his own determinate thought processes, and indeed the very forms of the problems from which he set forth, limits the results of his thinking. For the Marxist dialectic, on the other hand, the self-consciousness aimed at is the awareness of the thinker's position in society and in history itself, and of the limits imposed on this awareness by his class position—in short of the ideological and situational nature of all thought and of the initial invention of the problems themselves. (*Marxism*, 340)

Clearly, Berthoff's pedagogy of knowing is more thoroughly worked out on Hegelian terms of self-knowledge than Marxian terms of historical knowledge. Meaning-making remains, in Berthoff's lexicon, an unproblematized term; students are not invited to examine its various functions within the academic project. In that sense, the making of meaning remains an idealism even as it is intended to signify processes that subvert essential knowledge and fixed meanings. Miller speaks to this point when she writes that social process theorists have embraced the concept of the social construction of meaning without attending to its implications for the politics of student writing. "This further political contextualization of student writing . . . has not been fully accomplished in any view of process," she writes (112). And while she denies a subversive intention, Miller argues for precise historical awareness among students of the discourses they use while in the process of learning to write: "I am not suggesting that the proper application of social process theories would end in talking student out of the desires . . . to learn institutional conventions. . . . The issue is what they will learn *about* such conventions" (112). I will explore this issue at length in chapters 4 and 5.

For now we can say that dialectical self-consciousness is a varied capacity that may, but does not have to, stop at the point of Hegelian insight, where the contingency of meaning is discovered. For students brought to this point, tremendous insight may obtain, which over time may lead to the kinds of questions Freire and Miller raise about the social and historical nature of thought and writing: Why are certain perspectives and conventions valued more than others? Or, why are certain contexts and styles more easily imagined than others? Surely, some students will use the dialectic of composing that they learn in a way that reinvents historical materialism. It is also possible to teach this hermeneutic method deliberately.

III

In the conclusion of the first section, I outlined the goals of an interpretive method based on principles of critical effectivity. Briefly stated, these goals include (1) restoring a cultural artifact to the social dialogue it is part of so as (2) to understand the specific hegemonic relations that structure the dialogue, and thereby to enable one (3) to read an artifact's form ideologically as a specific way of representing the world. The principles of critical effectivity further presuppose that a student's writing and the processes used to generate it also be seen as an artifact worthy of comparable analysis. In this way, the incessant quality of ideological recognition that Althusser discusses can be put into action, thus substituting the idealism of conclusive critical knowledge with a process of continuous critique.

In this section, the writings of various students are discussed in an effort to explore the implications of critical effectivity for composition pedagogy and research. In the first set of papers, three students work with the concepts of dialectical thinking, social contradiction, and cultural hegemony in an incremental way that enables them to see and feel how these concepts complement and improve their own thinking processes rather than replace them. In these papers, the students were working with John Berger's critical essays on art in *About Looking* (1980).

To begin their work, these students were asked to write about a picture of a man's suit not only because of its obvious semiotic richness, but because of a particular essay in Berger's book, "The Suit and the Photograph." In this essay, Berger restores August Sander's 1914 photograph, "Peasants Going to a Dance," to its social and historical context in such a way as to define the specific hegemonic relations that shape the way the peasants "look" in their suits. What Berger is particularly interested in is the physical contradiction between the peasants' bodies "which are fully at home in effort" and their suits. As a ruling-class costume originating in Europe in the nineteenth century, the suit, Berger argues, was intended "to idealise purely sedentary power," and thus came to look normal on the corpulent bodies of those who administered (34). The fact that peasants and workers adopted these costumes as their own for formal occasions is, as Berger puts it, an "easily taught example of class hegemony" (35).

As "easily taught" as this example of cultural hegemony may be, it nevertheless constituted the final text of a two-week project. Before this, students did much writing and rewriting about suits, so that Berger's text might help them to complete analyses they had begun, analyses whose gaps could be filled once the concepts of contradiction and hegemony were found. One student wrote at length about the various ways she had thought about suits—in terms of her love for her father, in terms of funerals and death, in terms of her ambivalent feelings about a man's attractiveness in a suit, and in terms of the way suits, as symbols of male success, exclude women. She wrote the following about what she had learned:

> Before I embarked on this series of assignments, I had never given much conscious thought to the concept of the suit. I hadn't spent time investigating my feelings or associations in relation to suits, what they mean to me, what they mean to other people. . . . One of the most exciting points that became clearly illuminated for me in this process is how many thoughts can surface and evolve simply through looking, writing and looking again, then writing some more. I would not have imagined that I could spend two weeks on this process of thinking and writing about something as mundane as a man's suit. I became aware that through this method of attention and probing, anything from a candlestick to a lampshade or a flower vase offers this potential for the discovery of all kinds of meanings which seemed not to have existed before, at least consciously.

To be sure, if the project had stopped with these insights, it would have been of some value in the way it shows students how "writing dialectically encourages as it *requires* conscientization." By pursuing a dialogue with suits, the writer and her classmates were in a position to recognize themselves as makers of meaning, finding "all kinds of meanings which seemed not to have existed before." On the other hand, it seems hard to imagine a passage of student writing that better reflects an "almost entirely formalist and intransitive vision" of the writing process "for-its-own sake" (Miller, 1991: 97). The project, however, did not stop at this intransitive stage; it included a more dialectical and materialist phase of insight and analysis which the writer above actually mentions in the second sentence where there is an ellipsis. The beginning along with the completed second sentence reads as follows: "Before I embarked on this series of suit assignments . . . I hadn't spent time investigating my feelings or associations in relation to suits, what they mean to me, what they mean to other people, when and how they originated and how and why they're worn." Once the students read Berger and started rereading and rewriting their notebook entries in terms of his questions, the whole project advanced dialectically. Berger's interest in such questions as when and how suits originated and how and why they were worn initiated for the students a new phase of dialogue with their ideas about suits. In this phase, the students were struggling to make sense of Berger's concepts—a virtually new language—in terms of their own experience and their own language. One student worked through analogy:

> By the time August Sander began his series of photographic "archtypes," the suit was a definite part of the peasant/worker life. What Berger is ultimately trying to tell us is that the suit had very little context in either of their lives. It had become part of their life, he claims, through "class hegemony." The lower classes "came to accept *as their own*, standards of chic and sartorial worthiness." And in doing so "condemned them[selves] within the system of those standards, to being always, and recognisably to the classes above them, second rate, clumsy, uncouth, defensive." In other words, you should stick with the loose, comfortable peasant

garb and leave the suits to the sedentary or at least to the wealthy and powerful.
And doesn't this fashion elitism still exist in a far more subtle yet pervasive way? The new fall fashions worn by Harvard and BU students from wealthy backgrounds will be "knocked off," copied by a company in Korea or Hong Kong and put on the shelves next fall at some discount store in a mall and bought by the lower middle class kids going to Framingham State. These kids will in turn be scoffed at by those Harvard kids for wearing cheap imitations of last year's "hot" clothes. Maybe Mao best understood the interaction between fashion and class when he had eight hundred million Chinese wear the exact same uniform.

In this excerpt, the student is concerned with understanding the meaning of hegemony as the lived experience of class contradiction. He looks for a current example of such contradiction in fashion and finds it in the sportswear wars among his peers. Interestingly, he seems more drawn to the concepts than to the object of study, suits, and has found his way into his subject by renaming the governing idea for himself as "fashion elitism." Particularly compelling here is the decisive translation of cultural hegemony into precise terms—"knocked off," "cheap imitations," " 'hot' clothes"—terms that establish the example as both continuous with and different from Berger's. Reading fashion elitism in the language through which it is represented, the writer is able to avoid simplistic or deterministic thinking. His depiction retains its historical specificity and, as such, its overdetermined quality. By virtue of this overdetermined specificity, the writer has initiated a *new* dialectic in regard to his key term, *class hegemony*: the dialectic of past significance and present meaning (Weimann, 1976: 9). This dialectic enacts the incessant, re-historicizing quality of critical effectivity.
In another excerpt, it is possible to see a student rethinking an incident involving jackets after reading Berger. Similar to the preceding writer, she paraphrases the Berger essay first in order to set up her example, which I am including here with only the final sentence of the prior paragraph:

The suit draws attention to the peasants' position because their bodies make a statement about themselves that they cannot disguise, and because of this, the suit cannot make successfully its statement about privilege and an easy life. Today suits and jackets are required by some restaurants and clubs as part of the dress code. I think sometimes the men that wear these jackets feel that their clothing makes a statement about themselves. A friend and I were denied admission to one of these clubs because he was not wearing a jacket at the time. We changed our plans and went to a club that didn't require jackets and had a very good time. Weeks later, however, when I mentioned to my friend that I wanted to go shopping for myself, he cautiously remarked that he'd like to go with me. He said he'd been meaning to go shopping for a suit jacket: I couldn't believe that he was still feeling awkward about that night! Obviously, he felt that he did not belong, or was not good enough to be admitted to the club, and that as a result I felt the same way. Somewhat like Berger's peasants, my friend wanted to be a "member of the club," he didn't want to be inferior anymore. So even today, in an allegedly classless society, class hegemony still exists.

Because this example comes from a personal experience, it is possible to see quite vividly how the writer restores the dialogue to an event about whose meaning it could also be said she had been "denied admission." Now, however, rather than not knowing, that is, rather than taking the incident at face value, she rereads it in terms that examine the said and the not-said dialectically and problematically: "Weeks later . . . when I mentioned to my friend that I wanted to go shopping for myself, he cautiously remarked that he'd like to go with me. . . . I couldn't believe he was still feeling awkward about that night! Obviously, he felt that . . . he was not good enough to be admitted to that club."

Interpreting her friend's silences and cautious speech in terms of his feelings of inferiority, the writer is now in a position to avoid the two most obvious responses to this problem. One would be to sincerely regret the effects of this particular individual's "inferiority complex," and the second would be to sincerely regret the unfair ways of the world. Instead, she is able (in this writing) to go beyond a language of individualism and a language of condolence about the way things are because she has begun to learn a language with which she can analyze the way things are. Reading her essay through the framework of critical effectivity, we can appreciate (rather than denounce) the paradox of this passage's incisiveness *and* superficiality. For instance, the throwaway final sentence hints at the writer's discomfort with the knowledge her reading has produced. Discomfort, though not an end in itself, is a strong sign of a student writing transitively about *something* in particular. Possibly she never expected to find a place in her own thinking for the available cliché, "allegedly classless society," whose sources in left-wing discourse she does not altogether trust. Or possibly she finds the serious implications of her conclusions somewhat ahead of her intellectual commitments. Whatever the case, the theory of critical effectivity presumes a measure of nonidentity between one's writing and one's subjectivity, and as such it invites us to read these dissonances as part and parcel of social dialectics. This pedagogical response to contradiction in student writing is entirely different from the pedagogical response to such writing when it is taught as an entirely formal and intransitive process. In that case, coherence, defined as the virtual identity between one's writing and one's subjectivity, is presumed to be the goal.

If the students in these two excerpts show what critical work in its effects looks like as they practice dialogical restoration and the reading of hegemonic forms, the writer in the following excerpt shows what it looks like to work these dialectical ways of thinking into a more sustained discourse. Dialectical thinking, Jameson has written, involves not only reflection on our thoughts, but also their "fulfillment" (1974: 341) through the discovery that "all events carry their own logic, their own 'interpretations' within themselves" (345). This important point carries us back to Althusser's conviction that to realize Marx's discoveries we must read each particular contradictory result of social life not as the expression of some ultimate truth, but as a necessary and contingent production whose logic is as historically specific as the result itself. When we think dialectically to the point of discovering such contingency, it can feel like whiplash, a sudden reverse motion at which point questions become answers, problems become solutions. In the following excerpt, the writer swings around each paragraph dialectically, in order to explore how the contradictory conditions she examines may "carry their own logic":

> While some aspects of the suit as a fashion and a symbol of formality, authority and success have remained constant since its conception in the late 1800s, other aspects of it have undergone transformations with the development of new values and perspectives, and the shifting of old ones. The nature of class hegemony and people's response to it that Berger illustrates in his essay through the suit, seem to have altered. In the case that Berger presents, peasants blindly accepted standards set by the ruling class. Consequently, peasants looked clumsy and ill-proportioned in the suits developed by the ruling class. . . . Conversely, the ruling class "gentlemen" were physically flattered by the fit of this costume which they developed. Peasants were generally speaking much more fit and better proportioned than the ruling class because of their physical lifestyle. Because of this, it seemed they *should* have looked better in whatever they wore. This physicality, however, was not what the suit was designed for. Yet as Berger and the photograph portray, the peasants and country men did not *feel* clumsy wearing their suits but wore them with pride and felt well-dressed in them. This fact seemed to be caused by the unquestioning acceptance of ruling class standards and a lack of awareness that what was good for the ruling class was not necessarily suitable for them.
>
> Today a fashion of the suit has developed which has many characteristics in common with the way peasants wore their suits. The peasants however did not choose this particular formless fashion to be "hip" or stylish. This ill-fitted oversized look of suits which I am referring to *is* very specifically and consciously chosen by people, i.e., young people, of today. This anomaly could be indicative either of a decrease in the class hegemony Berger refers to, or simply of an altered response to it. While the "ruling class" no longer sets the trends in fashion and no longer is blindly accepted as the ultimate authority of standards in general, the element of rebellion to their standards as exemplified in this purposely

contradictory suit style may in fact illustrate the enduring presence of class hegemony.

In each paragraph, the writer finds the logic of a contradiction in terms of hegemonic relations. In each paragraph, she swings herself around so as to see a conflict as a relationship, a problem as a solution within historically specific limits. Reading the effects of history in social relations, she is reading dialectically. Like the other students, she eschews the common-sense response for one that reads for the origins and functions of such contradictory relations: "This anomaly could be indicative either of a decrease in the class hegemony Berger refers to, or simply of an altered response to it."

Once students have practiced restoring a cultural artifact to the specific hegemonic relations it is part of, they are in a position to "see" ideology in representations of the world—their own and others'. However, as we observed in an earlier section, one tendency in composition studies has been to privilege a student's own subjectivity from the framework of social interpretation, and this is evident in the above passages on Berger's essay. In each case, the students have construed the assignment as an invitation to divulge the contradictions and anomalies of others while remaining, themselves, outside the hegemonic circle. Dialectics, even social dialectics, can quickly take the tint of formalist problem solving. One can indeed imagine going from suits to ties to lampshades to candlesticks producing social analyses about "nothing in particular." On the other hand, one can avoid eliciting laundry lists of social mythologies by working with students to develop their methods for understanding ideology's mechanisms, not just its effects. Althusser alludes to this dynamic when he says that the "incessant practice of ideological recognition" is not enough. Along with such practice, we need a "knowledge of the mechanism of this recognition" (*Lenin*, 173).

In *About Looking* John Berger goes beyond recognition of ideology's effects on peasants as represented in Sander's photograph to a more theoretical essay on the uses of photography itself. He analyzes the mechanisms of photography's effects, thereby supplying a practical method for students as well. Borrowing from Susan Sontag, he argues that the free-standing public photograph in newspapers and magazines denies context and continuity, thereby rendering individual moments mysterious (49). "The task of an alternative photography," he writes, "is to incorporate photography into social and political memory, instead of using it as a substitute which encourages the atrophy of such memory" (58). In that way, the public photographer is not outside the events, seizing them mechanically, but rather "a recorder for those involved" (58). Citing a memorial display of Russian war photographs from 1941 to 1945, Berger explores their unglorifying, unspectacular qualities. Unlike most public photography which is unilinear in meaning—one stark image, one main idea—these photographs are radial in what they depict, for example: a young woman reading by flame, head down on her arms, while men and women sleep in the background, ragged, bandaged, rifles poised. By implication, the photographer himself is part of the story—a participant, along with the reading woman in a different form of resistance. Berger writes:

> There is never a single approach to something remembered. The remembered is not like a terminus at the end of a line. Numerous approaches or stimuli converge and lead to it. Words, comparisons, signs need to create a context for a printed photograph in a comparable way; that is to say, they must mark and leave open diverse approaches. A radial system has to be constructed around the photograph so that it may be seen in terms which are simultaneously personal, political, economic, dramatic, everyday and historic. (62–63)

This list, simple as it appears, provides a complex set of perspectives for restoring an artifact to its context along with one's place in relation to that context. As such, it offers a mechanism for ideological recognition. What Berger does not make explicit here (as he does elsewhere) is that by constructing a radial presentation or by deconstructing one through radial analysis, a reader inevitably encounters contradiction and overdetermination—the multiple, conflictual relations among these aspects of experience.

For example, in his essay, "Photographs of Agony," in *About Looking*, Berger discusses how the easy accessibility of a universal perspective on suffering exists at the expense of economic or historic perspectives that would provide access to the sources of that suffering. Students who learn to work dialectically with perspec-

The Dialectic since Marx 35

tives—in the manner of Berger—may come to see that taking a universal perspective tends, in Western tradition, to subvert an economic or historic perspective. With this experience, it is not easy to remain neutral to the meaning of these approaches. They do not simply constitute a plurality, a banquet of options. As forms of knowledge, their relations are conflictual and hegemonic.

The meaning of these forms of relations thus comes under scrutiny in a radial approach, which supplies the mechanisms for ideological recognition. The intransitive role of the student writer who would accumulate meanings under the rubric of multiple perspective becomes more difficult to sustain uncritically. No longer privileged as outside the circle of hegemonic relations, a student's own forms of representation can be felt against the skin, like the rough wool of a peasant's suit. And when the writing process itself can be felt and seen as a social and historical source of meaning, interesting effects in the writing can be observed as in the example that follows:

Irish Lass, 6, Crosses Ocean

Chatting in the lilting tones of Ireland, her grey eyes big with wonderment, her little sailorman doll clutched tightly in her hand and a sausage-like balloon tucked carefully under her arm, Mary E. Harney, 6-year-old adventurer, landed in America today after looking on Boston from the deck of the Cunard-White Star liner *Laconia* as a fairy city.

Motherless, the little Irish lass has been living with her father, James. But James had five children, and money in Athlone was not easy to come into possession of, so it was decided that Mary should visit her aunt in Boston for a good long stay.

The above excerpt from the October 6, 1936, *Boston Traveler* is part of an entire page of newspaper accompanying one student's essay about her mother's emigration. A radial examination, Gerri G.'s essay explores not only the newspaper story itself, but also its relation to the accompanying photograph and other stories on the page. Problematizing the large personal interest story in relation to other more briefly reported events—such as a meeting between

Mussolini's son-in-law, Galeazzo Ciano, and Hitler's foreign minister, Konstantin von Neurath—she discovers something about the politics of the "human interest" feature and her own choices as a writer. On page three of her essay, Gerri begins to read against the grain of the feature, and she continues by asking questions of herself that are implied by her critique:

> Mary was not an adventurer at all. The writer's language quite clearly defies any such connotations of adventurousness in the child's journey, which in reality "was decided" for her by unfortunate circumstances of death and economic poverty, whereby she was consequently "put aboard the steamer." Furthermore, the "visit" to her aunt was undoubtedly intended to be more than "a good long stay" though, conceivably this may have been the story told to Mary. Nevertheless, my mother never saw or heard from her father again and was not to see her four siblings until 37 years later.
>
> The misrepresentation of reality in the *Traveler's* photojournalistic "human interest story," created out of the facts surrounding my mother's emigration to the United States, is comparable to Berger's evaluation of the contemporary public photograph. He writes:
>
> The contemporary public photograph usually presents an event, a seized set of appearances, which has nothing to do with us, its readers, or with the original meaning of the event. (52)
>
> Therefore I must ask myself: To what purpose did the "seized set of appearances"—a child sitting on her trunk holding a doll and balloon serve for the *Boston Traveler's* journalist and photographer in October of 1936? And further, can I, more than fifty-one years after the moment the photographer's flashbulb blinded six year old Mary's vision, restore any personal truth to the layers of reality submerged within the artificiality of the news story?

These powerful questions characterize critical effectivity. First, the author poses a question that will historicize the contradictions she has observed: "What purpose did the 'seized set of appearances' . . . serve?" Next, she wonders whether further work with this story might make it useful to her own developing sense of self: "Can I ... restore any personal truth" to the story, she asks. As the author proceeds to examine the ideological effects of the feature, using the mechanisms she has learned, a dialectic between the languages of historical analysis and "personal truth" ensues. This process begins in the passage below where Gerri attempts to develop an historical understanding of the disproportionate stories she is studying. She dismisses the value-free, ahistorical explanation that the feature's greater length is a result of its simply being "more interesting" than the Ciano/von Neurath meeting. At the start, her style of explanation is somewhat elliptical, suggesting the difficulty she is having bringing together the conventionally disparate forms of knowledge and levels of history that she has researched. As she continues, the author makes her observations about these two stories relevant to the "selecting and prioritizing of reportable events." In a later passage, this point of emphasis leads the author to problematize her *own* ways of "selecting and prioritizing" the events surrounding her mother's emigration. In this way, the personal becomes historical too. The first passage reads as follows:

> In 1936, the year my grandmother died in Ireland and my mother emigrated to America, the Spanish Civil War erupted and the "joint Italo-German warfare on communism" involved direct military support of Franco's Nationalists. The governments of both the United States and the fledgling Irish Republic remained officially detached from the war in Spain.
> Two years after Mussolini's son-in-law and Reichfuehrer Hitler discussed "questions dealing with the Austro-German pact" the German army marched into Austria unopposed and Hitler spoke triumphantly to a group of 400 members of the Nazi press corps:
>> One fundamental factor must be recognized: the press, gentlemen, can achieve incredible things and can exert an incredible influence whenever it serves as a means to an end. (Hauner 135)
>
> In the 1930's, Hitler adroitly manipulated not only the Nazi press, but the world press as well, extolling his "Peace Plan" while simultaneously rebuilding the German military; a ploy

alarmingly analogous to the Reagan Administration's fervent ideological justification of "Star Wars" as a potential for peace achieved through strength. The selection and prioritizing of reportable events determined by the editors of the 1936 *Boston Traveler*, suggests that the American press, or at least factions thereof, avoided politicizing, within the broad American consciousness, the volatile situation in Europe. . . . What I find to be personally offensive is the *Traveler's* opportunistic use of a traumatic event in my mother's childhood as a public spectacle, skirting reality and skewing the facts to fit a shallow, fictitious fairy tale.

In this passage, Gerri's radial practice helps her to focus more and more on the history and politics of a story's representation. As a result, the pressure appears to build for her to reflect on her *own* practice. Can she respond to the *Traveler*'s story without idealizing her own writing process as neutral, disinterested, or simply personal? As she poises herself to present her version of Mary Harney's story, Gerri seems to be trying to find a function as a writer which does not, willy-nilly, turn her mother into another kind of "public spectacle": the object of her true vision. As stated earlier, the theory of critical effectivity presupposes that knowledge of one's subjectivity cannot be learned in the fixed manner of a history lesson but rather must be understood over and over again in its effects. Despite the temptation for this writer to conceive her subjectivity in traditional, ahistorical terms as the restorer of truth, it would seem that the mechanism of ideological recognition which she has used to deconstruct the relationship among the *Traveler* articles is also having its effects on her relationship to her own writing. In what follows, Gerri acknowledges, implicitly, that she, too, is selecting and prioritizing and that her purposes are not value-free. For instance, she does not say that she is facing reality or straightening out the facts; she says instead that she is using writing as an agent for values *different* from the ones shaping the feature. She does not purport to be presenting the true story; rather, she writes:

I want to propose a *contrary image* of my mother's arrival in the United States and would like to borrow Berger's words again as my rationale, my right and indeed my obligation to do so. He writes:

> If the living take the past upon themselves, if the past becomes an integral part of the process of people making their own history, then all photographs would reacquire a living context. (57, emphasis mine)

As the agent for the recontextualization of her mother's story, Gerri consciously mediates between past meaning and present significance. Thus, her notion of a "contrary image" does not mean the opposite or "true" image, but rather, an image of her mother's subjectivity which permits her to act on behalf of her own subjectivity. Not surprisingly, she gives priority to her mother's gender and order of birth in her "contrary image":

> *I* believe that my mother sat atop her trunk after emerging from the Cunard-White Star Liner Laconia clutching not merely a sailor doll and balloon, but a profound, unendurable sorrow. There is no imaginable reason or enticement that could have persuaded a six year old child to willingly leave her home and board a mammoth ship headed for a foreign country.
>
> My mother was sent to live with her aunt not only because of the death of her mother and the poverty suffered by her family but also because of her particular position in her family, in relation to her age and gender. She was the fourth child in the family, having an older sister, Sarah, the first born, after whom there were two older brothers, Peter and Daniel, and finally an infant sister, Kathleen, who was born shortly before their mother's death. Obviously, their father James needed the two boys to help on the farm, and of course he likely held traditional patriarchal values that placed a higher esteem upon "Erin's" sons than daughters. More significantly, Sarah's labor was needed for cooking, caring for the infant and in general for all the household chores previously performed by their mother. Thus, it must have been painfully decided that six year old Mary, being more of an economic burden than asset to the survival of a family in the midst of a

worldwide depression, should go to live with a financially secure aunt in America.

In this reading, Mary's insignificance, in terms of her gender and birth order, led to her separation from her family. By naming the contradictory and overdetermined historical processes that contributed not only to the *Traveler*'s but also her family's forms of selecting and prioritizing, Gerri has done more than just clarify what she calls her "nebulous" sense of her mother's youth. In her essay, she reads past representations critically in order to act in the present in a way that is *not* "nebulous." In short, as a writer she generates a new artifact. This is especially significant inasmuch as no personal artifacts of her mother's youth survived Mary Harney's split from her aunt:

> My mother cooked, cleaned and cared for her aunt, whom I never met, until deciding, at the age of 24, to marry and move away. This decision was not well received, nor supported, by the elderly aunt and within a few months a painful, permanent separation ensued; a split so abrupt and final that it meant the leaving behind of all mementoes: photographs, school report cards, yearbooks, letters, scrapbooks, everything connected with the piece of life my mother had lived with this aunt.
>
> Thus, my own sense of my mother's youth is nebulous. I have only this image from the newspaper, which my mother retrieved from the archives of the Boston Public Library a few years ago.

By adding to the artifacts about Mary Harney's youth, Gerri participates in the process that critical effectivity describes: she has analyzed various hegemonic discourses about her mother's emigration and produced a representation of her mother's youth which she believes does not serve those same interests in the same way. By virtue of this process, she has re-seen an aspect of her own subjectivity in ways that affect her actions in the present. Learning to think about the sources of her own and others' thought conscientiously and problematically, this writer is engaged in a process informed by the question, "What is it to read?"

The Dialectic since Marx

In *Postmodern Education* (1991), Henry Giroux works with the concept of reterritorialization as he builds a definition of what a critical pedagogy of reading and writing would entail. His metaphor of territory (borrowed from Caren Kaplan) recalls Althusser's metaphor of terrain in that both are geographical terms used by their authors to emphasize the way dialectical thought provides new grounding for knowledge. Giroux writes that although a student's experience should be "confirmed," it should also be "critically interrogated"–that is, "remade, reterritorialized in the interest of a social imaginary that dignifies the best traditions and possibilities of those groups who are learning to speak from a discourse of dignity and self-governance" (129).

In her representation of Mary Harney's story, the author of the above essay has not simply corrected the superficialities of the *Traveler* story with new facts; she has problematized the feature, analyzed the forces that would motivate the rendering of some stories superficially and others deeply, and then rewritten it. Engaged by a pedagogy that offers her a mechanism for ideological recognition, she investigates and then reterritorializes the story. Such a pedagogy, Giroux writes, "replaces the authoritative language of recitation with an approach that allows students to speak from their own histories, collective memories, and voices while simultaneously challenging the grounds on which knowledge and power are constructed and legitimated" (130). In the next chapter, we will look at the philosophy of language developed by M. M. Bakhtin in relation to the issue of replacing the authoritative languages of recitation with languages that are "internally persuasive" and open to dialogue.

THREE

Toward Internally Persuasive Discourse Effects: Working Bakhtin's Theory of Language

> Both the authority of discourse and its internal persuasiveness may be united in a single word.... But such unity is rarely a given—it happens more frequently that an individual's becoming, an ideological process, is characterized precisely by a sharp gap between these two categories.
>
> —Mikhail Bakhtin, *The Dialogic Imagination*

I

In the preceding chapter, Henry Giroux is cited as recommending that authoritative pedagogies based on recitation be replaced with approaches that invite students both to confirm and to interrogate their experiences. Such a pedagogy would require students to explore the ways authoritative discourses have shaped their understanding of their experiences. This exploratory process by which one works toward new, internally persuasive relations with languages depends on an understanding of why these authoritative discourses hold such high status (and why others do not). Through such understanding, the authoritative languages that may claim significant roles in our thought processes are not so much replaced as opened up (to some degree) for dialogic review and reterritorialization. This uneven but ongoing review constitutes what Bakhtin calls "the ideological becoming of a human being . . . [which] is the process of selectively assimilating the words of others"

(1981: 341). This ongoing review also characterizes the theory of critical effectivity that we have been pursuing. As such, Bakhtin's philosophy of language, in particular its emphasis on the struggle involved in understanding the relations among languages, can give finer grain to the theory of critical effectivity.

Bakhtin's philosophy of language is founded on the principles of heteroglossia and dialogism: "at any given moment in its historical existence, language is heteroglot from top to bottom," stratified by different classes, races, genders, ages, professions, families, locales, and more. Furthermore, the interactions among these languages are constantly constructing new socially typifying languages (291). These languages do have one thing in common, Bakhtin stresses: they are all "specific points of view on the world, forms for conceptualizing the world in words" (291–92). And because language is always a "concrete heteroglot conception of the world" (293), one's language, one's individual consciousness is always already saturated by the otherness of living language, the language as it "exists in other people's mouths, in other people's contexts, serving other people's intentions: it is from there that one must take the word, and make it one's own" (294).

For Bakhtin, in other words, all our discourse is already social through and through, already in dialogue. "Only the mythical Adam," whose word and whose world were verbally unqualified, was free of the internal dialogism of the word (279). The rest of us, structured by historical human discourse, continue to structure what we know and how we know it within this polyglot language environment.

How then, we must ask along with Bakhtin, can one create a language of "one's own" given the social nature of language? The answer, it would seem, lies not in some effort to carve out for oneself an autonomous realm of language free from sociality, but rather to become a more knowing participant in the social dialogue that constitutes all discourse, with ourselves and others. Bakhtin refers to this knowing participation in the social dialogue as "relativized consciousness" (324). Although no person or group can ever really be free of the social chorus within, whole groups of people may live as if they are. For such groups, multi-voicedness is lived as predetermined shifts, not as thought processes. Under such circumstances, dialogic interorientation is automatic: "There is no attempt," Bakhtin writes, "to look at one of these languages through the eyes of another language" (295). Like Paulo Freire after him, Bakhtin links the ability to look relatively at one's movement among languages with the possibility for political action and awareness. Both link literacy to the struggle for social justice through the creative process by which a person comes into dialogical consciousness of conflicting languages for conceptualizing the world. Speaking of the illiterate Russian peasantry in the early twentieth century, Bakhtin wrote that only when a "critical interanimation of languages" began to occur, only as it became clear that the ideological systems of these languages were in contradiction and could not coexist peacefully—only then the "predetermined quality of these languages came to an end, and the necessity of actively choosing one's orientation among them began" (296).

In other words, consciousness of heteroglossia is a prerequisite for choosing one's own language orientation. Thus, imagination in a heteroglot world is always dialogical, always aware of multiple, conflicting meanings for the same things. A significant problem for practicing relativized consciousness is that these languages of heteroglossia are often authoritative and antidialogical: they prohibit questioning and interanimation. And despite Bakhtin's generalization regarding the predetermined shifts of whole groups, language relations can never be completely preformulated or socially typical because, as Caryl Emerson writes, "no two individuals ever entirely coincide in their experience or belong to precisely the same set of social groups" (1983: 248). Consequently, much imagination must be spent suppressing the recognition of conflict among these languages, these "points of view on the world."

Rather than characterizing these relations to authoritative discourse as passive and monologic (the absence of activity), as is Bakhtin's tendency, it might be more useful to see them *as* an activity, the activity of negative dialogics: the work of keeping authoritative discourse in place and away from the "zone of contact" (346). Indeed, Bakhtin's work would seem to support this reformulation. In an extended discussion of "passive understanding," for instance, he recognizes that the process by which one stays "within his own boundaries" is accomplished by concrete acts of attention—such as making efforts to be more clear, persuasive, and vivid within those boundaries (281). These efforts may be largely negative, but they are still responses to a perceived demand (281). Fending off dialogue, then, is in fact a kind of dialogue requiring material action.

When we understand that the maintenance of authoritative relations is itself a dialogical action (albeit negative), we cannot responsibly put forward a dialogical pedagogy based on the assumption that we are activating still minds with new techniques for ideological becoming. Every student is already in the process of ideological becoming by virtue of the ongoing actions that maintain and adjust the relations among one's languages. Bringing these actions forward for "relativization" is a theoretically responsible goal; activating still minds is not.

As such, Bakhtin's concept of internally persuasive discourse can help us to develop a pedagogy for fostering a fuller range of dialogic action in our students' writing. In his essay, "Discourse in the Novel," Bakhtin opposes internally persuasive discourse with authoritative discourse as if he were making a simple contrast between one's own language and the language of authority. However, he is not forming simple opposites in this way. Rather, he is proposing alterative forms of language relations: the former, dialectical and relativizing; the latter, binary and absolute. For Bakhtin, the internally persuasive word is not "ours" in any simple sense: it is "half-ours and half-someone else's" (345). Its personal persuasiveness derives from the work we are able to do with it: "[W]e can take it into new contexts, attach it to new material . . . in order to wrest new answers from it" (346). Glossing this important distinction in Bakhtin, Don Bialostosky has written that the internally persuasive word differs from the authoritative word "not so much as inner to outer" but as "answerable to unanswerable" (1991: 15).

If negative dialogics maintain certain discourses as unanswerable, the purpose of developing internally persuasive relations is to stimulate answer-ability. From this distinction we can take the following point: a pedagogy directed toward the cultivation of internally persuasive discourse is not the same thing as a pedagogy directed against authoritative discourse. In the former, we direct ourselves toward knowledge of the language relations we are in; in the latter, we would seek to divest them out of hand. As such, the second pedagogy would constitute another authoritative discourse, directed toward the affirmation or rejection of students' language relations.

Different in intent as well as in method, a pedagogy informed by the concept of internally persuasive language relations is not "directed toward" students at all. A pedagogy "directed toward" students could never be included as one of the objects of study, as we are suggesting it must be. What students learn about and do with their relationships to textual authority is indissoluble from what they learn about and do with their relationship to a teacher's authority. The struggle toward more internally persuasive relations inevitably engages both, for both are materialized in language. In each case, the work of the teacher is to create the conditions by which a student's own discourse may be "gradually and slowly wrought out of others' words that have been acknowledged and assimilated . . . the boundaries between the two [being] at first scarcely perceptible" (345).

For Bakhtin, assimilation does not mean uncritical acceptance of dominant languages and points of view. Rather, assimilation stands for the process by which a critical dialogue with others' words is undertaken precisely to avoid their passive absorption. Assimilation, then, is a relativizing procedure that creates the possibility for making choices among the languages of heteroglossia, choices based on difference and distance, not just identity. The dynamic required for this kind of response-ability is a particularly significant aspect of Bakhtin's philosophy.

Rejecting the Sausurrian dichotomy between *langue* and *parole*—language as social code and language as individual message—Bakhtin developed a model depicting the dialectical relationship between them. "In the Bakhtinian model," Caryl Emerson writes, "every individual engages in two perpendicular activities. He forms lateral ('horizontal') relationships with other individuals in specific speech acts and he simultaneously forms internal ('vertical') relationships between the outer world and his own psyche" (249). Through the constancy of these double activities, the social psyche develops. The extent to which this social psyche develops into an independent "ideological consciousness" depends on one's awareness of and one's capacity to exploit these double activities.

The role of the educator in this model is not hard to see. The educator creates the conditions under which students may study

(1) their lateral relationships with other individuals through speech acts and reader responses; and (2) the simultaneous vertical relationships between these social activities and their self-directed inner speech. Students who are studying these double activities may, for instance, analyze the heteroglossia in each others' writing toward more critical interanimation of these languages. Roughly speaking, this kind of activity works the dialectic from the horizontal to the vertical axis. It is also possible (and useful) to work the dialectic the other way—for instance, working with students to identify the influences and pressures leading their thought toward certain speech acts and written responses (and away from others). Both of these options are illustrated and discussed in the next section.

It would be a mistake, however, to overrate either of these moves as discrete, pedagogical actions. The ongoing dialogic sequence that comprises one's pedagogy is far more important to the cultivation of these double activities than the isolation of and preoccupation with particular instances of them. To be sure, composition classes must work closely with compositions. But the function of this work is ultimately a philosophical issue and not a commonsense one. Any response that a teacher makes to a student's writing should be framed by consideration of its role in the larger development of the student's internally persuasive discourse, in the context of a dialogical course sequence.

The kind of assignment sequencing we are talking about should privilege openness and play over formality and developmental process. The latter foci are likely to reinscribe sequencing into an authoritative discourse that permits little or no expansion of a student's range of dialogic action. The way in which sequenced assignments may undermine rather than support dialogic action has been observed by a number of theorists, including Ann Berthoff (1981) and John Clifford (1991). In a critique of the process approach to writing, Clifford observes the way sequenced writing assignments may actually contribute to a student's traditional role as the submissive subject of task work (the very kind of work that sequencing proponents have sought to avoid). Using anecdote to make this point pungently, Clifford writes:

> An instructor down the hall from me has turned composing into such a labrynthine sequence of prewriting heuristics,

drafts, revisions, and peer-editing sessions that she has probably truncated years of bureaucratic socialization into three months. With dozens of discrete steps and scores of self-interrogating, self-purifying questions about coherence devices and structuring techniques . . . she has validated the darkest epiphanies of Foucault and Althusser. (48)

To say the least, sequences that train students to adopt the current model of the academic writing process are not positioning students for relativized consciousness and knowing participation in their ideological becoming. No "composing process" pedagogy in its linear or developmental forms can. Finding one's own way by making choices among various dialogical options cannot really be modeled. The methods that Bakhtin names for stimulating internally persuasive discourse are not linear or developmental; they include recontextualization and interanimation because of the dialogizing effects they can have on one another (346). It is the double activities of discourse with others and discourse with ourselves that constitute the dynamics for a dialogical pedagogy. The way in which this dynamic may be applied to composition studies has been hinted at. In the next section, these matters are explored more thoroughly.

II

In composition studies today, it is common for scholars to perform Bakhtinian readings of student writing. In a recent example of this kind of article, Thomas Recchio analyzes the multiple discourses evident in a student's discussion of Freud's essay, "Taboo and the Ambivalence of Emotion."

Recchio writes that while working with his student his intention was to help her to name and objectify the discourses she employed so that she might assess the claims implicit in those discourses and compare them to Freud's. In so doing, Recchio writes, "[S]tudents are in a position to negotiate those claims as they work towards developing a consciously critical point of view on what they read through what they write" (1991: 447).

This procedure resembles the option discussed in the first section whereby students study the multiple discourses in their writing toward their critical interanimation and selective assimilation.

Recchio argues that his student cannot really develop an internally persuasive discourse in relation to Freud's concept of taboo without understanding the authoritative discourses she draws on to circumscribe Freud's text. He lists the three authoritative discourses his student draws upon as moral, pseudo-psychological, and Freudian (449–50). Notably, he identifies a fourth discourse—confessional narrative—but avoids discussing it because its ambiguity as a personal narrative about incest "presents special problems" (450).

Despite his useful application of Bakhtinian principles to the student essay, Recchio received sharp criticism for steering clear of the implicit narrative. The criticism took two forms: (1) that Recchio repressed the interanimation going on among the discourses; (2) that he disregarded the student's experiential discourse (Kramer, 1992; Tweedie, 1992). Because the first criticism raises important concerns for a pedagogy based on Bakhtinian principles and ultimately on the theory of critical effectivity which those principles support, it is discussed here at some length.

"Recchio's disregard for the decentralizing impulse [of the implied incest narrative] curtails the essay's heteroglossia," one respondent writes (Tweedie 1992: 527) Along with disregard, this respondent accuses Recchio of ignoring his own (Recchio's) earlier writing on the important role of narrative in a dialogic approach. The implication of the above criticism is this: if one does not apply every Bakhtinian principle, chapter and verse, in every situation, then one "subverts a Bakhtinian approach" (527). Of course, the fixed and dogmatic nature of this assumption goes completely against the grain of Bakhtinian thought, reifying it as an authoritative discourse that suffers no differences.

In this regard, it is important to remember that the interanimation of competing and conflicting discourses is not an end in itself. Another's ideological becoming is not something we take into our own hands, deciding where a little dialogic "tough love" might do some good. But the above respondent tips his hand in that direction when he writes, "I do not mean to seem insensitive ... I realize this situation is potentially explosive, just as Bakhtin's beloved carnival can be. But ... the undesired cannot be ignored away" (527). It is completely unclear what the respondent means by "potentially explosive"; with a sentimental analogy to Bakhtin's "beloved carnival" as his only gloss on the cliché, it would seem that he, too, wishes to avoid consideration of that fourth discourse's possible consequences. In short, the respondent's call for the full interanimation of conflicting discourses may be at the expense of the student's ideological becoming. Where such interanimation would threaten to silence a student (through "explosion," flight, or something in between), there is no justification for its pursuit—unless, that is, one mistakes the gradual, slow, and uneven process of becoming a more knowing participant in one's language relations with the U.S. Army's motto: "Be all that you can be."

This is not to say that one should not take the presence of an implied, confessional narrative seriously. Indeed, the function of a dialogically structured course sequence is to create the conditions for recontextualization and further interaction with suppressed discourses. Based neither on recursion nor revision per se (both of which posit timetables for growth and awareness), dialogical sequencing eschews the ideology of progress. The terms for "making progress" will always be another's: centralizing and authoritative. Because internally persuasive language relations initially represent efforts to distinguish oneself from the languages of authority, they are not likely to emerge forthrightly because they are assigned, but rather, they will appear tentatively, quizzically, associationally. Bakhtin writes that these relations are characterized by "a playing with distances, with fusion and dissolution, with approach and retreat" (343-44). Where the respondent above would assume that the place of the fourth, suppressed discourse is fully alongside the other three, a more dialectical reading of Bakhtin might suggest that the fourth discourse (in its struggle to become a more privileged internally persuasive discourse) might need distance from the other three and detachment from the Freud assignment to emerge for *gradual* interanimation and assimilation. The challenge for those who would design dialogic course sequences is much more to avoid canceling the possibility for accident and association, for approach and retreat, than it is to determine just when and how critical struggle with one's language relations should take place.

Unfortunately, there is no public documentation of the writing that followed Recchio's work with his student. Support for our hypothesis regarding the process of critical struggle must come from other sources. In a series of papers written by Rick L., a first-semester freshman at the University of Massachusetts–Boston, it is possible to observe in what ways and under what circumstances a student is able or not able to play with the authoritative language relations he is part of.

The first paper in the set of three to be considered was written midway into the semester in relation to "Our Time," a chapter from John Edgar Wideman's book, *Brothers and Keepers* (in Bartholomae and Petrosky, 1987). In that text, Wideman's "double activities" of dialogue with his brother, Robby, and dialogue with himself about his brother's words are directly represented. As a writer, Wideman worries that he is assimilating Robby's story too quickly, giving too little attention to the differences between Robby's language and his own language as a point of view. Raising this issue of languages as points of view and demonstrating the double activities that promote consciousness of it, Wideman's chapter invites students to pursue these concerns in their own contexts. the specific assignment generating Rick's paper asked students (1) to tell a story that included their own and at least one other person's perspective; and (2) to write about the experience of trying to listen to the other person's perspective.

In his essay, "The Experience," Rick describes driving from Boston to Cape Cod in a race with two other cars. He compares his view of the experience with those of the passengers in his car and the other cars. In the second of six paragraphs, Rick presents his point of view. A narrative comprising 50 percent of the essay, it is a heteroglot mélange of languages from various sources, including police reports, radio traffic reports, boys' adventure stories, sportscasting, and news analysis:

> I was one of the drivers on the trip down to the Cape that weekend. This ride would be considered a hell ride by most. There was a total of three cars driving down there that weekend and each was in a race with one another. I was determined to win no matter what the cost. Basically, all of the cars stayed at about 90 m.p.h. until we hit the rotary before the Bourne Bridge. This was designated as the take off point, and from there it was every man for themselves. The other two cars had about six of our friends in them. The exception was my car, I was carrying seven kids and the cooler (since my car was the

biggest). It could be said that each car had it's own cheering section for the driver. As we were approaching the bridge, while screaming back and forth from car to car, I could determine that there was a heavy backup due to the traffic. I didn't want to get slowed down by stopping for the traffic, so to gain some distance before the bridge—I sped up. The only problem with this was that the rotary came up on me faster than I had anticipated. I was driving between 110 and 120 m.p.h. when the bridge was about half a mile away. The only problem I had to face was there was traffic at a dead stop about 100 yards in front of me. I slammed on the brakes but the car still wasn't slowing down enough. Before I knew it, I was right on top of the traffic. I veered off into the dirt along the side of the road and kept going towards the bridge. I was passing the cars on the road to my right of me as if they were in reverse. When I was about 100 feet from the rotary, I had slowed down to about 60 m.p.h. I decided to jam on the horn and pray for the best while going around the rotary. I went around beeping the horn and my friends, who had already buckled their seatbelts, were screaming. With some amazing stroke of luck, I managed to make it from the rotary to the bridge without hitting anything of any major value. The car didn't actually make it around the rotary though. We drove just over the edge of it. We only hit a couple small shrubs, and uprooted a bed of flowers. We kept a reasonable speed until after the bridge and the traffic died down. Although by this time, we had a considerable lead over the other two cars. So after the bridge, I sped up to about 100 m.p.h., there wasn't any reason for any ridiculous speed because of the lead we had, and we made it to the cottage in record time. Eventually, the other two cars pulled up in front of the cottage and the party started. This was my viewpoint of the story. However, everyone else seemed to have their own version of how the ride actually took place.

The contradictory languages in this narrative do not appear to be a problem for the writer. He is able to call on languages of reason and superstition, of agency and fate, alternately, even interchangeably. For instance, driving 110 to 120 mph, he describes the traffic stopped 100 yards away as "The only problem I had to face." However, when he cannot slow down fast enough, he shifts to a magical discourse: "Before I knew it I was right on top of the traffic." Either phrase could begin either sentence. Struggling to frame his story for adult readers, Rick calls on any linking phrase he can to confer on his narrative what Bakhtin calls "pseudo-objective motivation" (305). In comic novels, the kinds of linking phrases we see here—"the only problem"; "before I knew it"; "with some amazing stroke of luck"—are used to mark out two speakers: the one who identifies with the objectivity of these phrases and the one who parodies them. Where these constructions are not consciously dialogized, they are only unintentionally comical.

Despite the incommensurability of these phrases, the paragraph shifts from one to the other smoothly and familiarly until the end when there is a noticeable breakdown in the capacity of linking and other phrases to maintain even pseudo-narrative coherence. The following sentence stands out in this regard: "So after the bridge, I sped up to about 100 m.p.h., there wasn't any reason for any ridiculous speed." What might be named as *the* authoritative rejoinder to his story—"There wasn't any reason for any ridiculous speed"—has been called on to serve his own context (no matter how awkwardly) in a strong example of negative dialogics. Trying to assimilate this rejoinder as his own, Rick only draws attention to the way that it has not yet been seen as a point of view he can look at, consider, and even dispute.

In the rest of the essay, as Rick reviews his friends' perspectives, he never goes beyond this method of containment. Recounting the rage of his passengers, Rick says he has come to realize "that what had just happened was somewhat dangerous." Two sentences later, he glosses "somewhat dangerous" with the observation, "I hadn't realized that I had taken my friends' life into my own hands." And in the conclusion of his essay when he describes how the passengers of his car refused to ride home with him, he writes, "I told them that I realized what had happened and agreed not to go over 100 m.p.h. But to this day, there are still a couple of my friends that refuse to get into the car with me."

Implicit in his conclusion is the authoritative notion that there was no reason for any ridiculous speed. When attached to a maximum speed of 100 mph, however, it is the realization that seems ridiculous. For Rick, however, the unmediated attachment of these authoritative standards of behavior to his own actions constitutes a perfect solution. He claims the standards as "his own" (with an air of bravado and possibly parody) while never having to address them directly. They remain absolute. As such, Rick appears to be experienced with the generative power of negative dialogics. However, he does not supply us with much evidence that he has ever struggled directly with the assumptions of an authoritative discourse or questioned its power to frame his thinking.

When a student is as engaged as Rick is by the generative power of negative dialogics, virtually any analysis of his containment strategies is likely to motivate new ones, at least for a while. Assigned revisions in such a case will be received as an order to divest oneself of one's old currency and to invest in the classroom form of exchange. Thus, in the assigned revision that followed this essay by a few weeks, the only modification in Rick's paper was a new conclusion that transferred the classroom discussion about his first draft onto the second. In that classroom discussion, students were asked to look at Rick's long second paragraph in relation to his claim at the end of the paper that he had seen the experience as "a controlled situation." Through our work, the various languages and conflicting points of view that he martials to narrate his side of the story were named and compared with this idea that the race had been a "controlled situation." Rick's revision (beginning with "Also") contains an accurate representation of that discussion:

> The entire time while I was listening to these stories, I was in a state of amazement. It was hard for me to believe what had just happened was dangerous. During this experience, I was thinking to myself that I had the situation totally under control. However, listening to the similarity of all these stories made me realize that what had just happened was somewhat dangerous. Also I realized after that the reason I could have felt that I had total control was because I was driving the car. Which even when I thought about it, I still wasn't in control. In fact, now that I look back, praying for the best doesn't sound like someone who was in total control. I realized that I had almost no control which way the car would travel. What I mean by this is that if I was going to crash, I had the choice

of which way to either hit a car or spin off the road. This feeling of control could have also been the fact that I was just mentally covering up the dangerous events that had just happened. Rather than admitting that I was in danger, I thought to myself that I was in charge of whatever happened to my friends and I.

It would seem that, to some extent, Rick's retelling of class discussion as his own thought process instigates a thought process. His assumption of control is looked at on its own terms ("total control" versus "almost no control"), and then it is looked at on psychological terms as a defense ("just mentally covering up the dangerous events"). However, the syntactical disarray of the revised sentences indicates unresolved difficulty with the process. Moreover, the revised section is followed by exactly the same sentence that followed the unrevised draft: "These somewhat different perspectives of this experience were a bit enlightening." Just as Rick attaches an authoritative judgment of his speeding to his own decision not to drive over 100 mph ("There wasn't any reason for any ridiculous speed"), he attaches a brief dialogic revision to his otherwise undisturbed essay. In the context of this narrative, apparently, Rick relates to both monologic and dialogic discourse as primarily authoritative, regardless of their potential differences. This is not to say that the revision should not have been assigned. On the one hand, it is impossible to know what overdetermined meanings there were for the author as he wrote to himself that choosing between hitting a car or spinning off the road represents "almost no control" rather than "total control." On the other hand, there appears to be almost no way that such understanding, as it is so completely identified with authoritative values, can become internally persuasive. Rick's resistance to its becoming internally persuasive is evident in his snarled syntax and his retention of the grudging judgment: "a bit enlightening."

It is arguable, as noted earlier, that the revision assignment has actually intensified the writer's difficulty in finding a place for himself among these conflicting discourses by seeming to require a direct confrontation between them. Rick responds to revision as part of an authoritative pedagogy based on acceptance or rejection. There is no indication that the author sees anything to do but to find a more acceptable place for himself within the authoritative dictum: "There wasn't any reason for any ridiculous speed." In the first draft, he attached his reduced speed of 100 mph to the dictum and found its reasonableness questioned. In the revision, he presents the class criticism of this reasoning as his own internal dialogue in a new act of assent to the larger moral judgment: "There wasn't any reason . . ."

On the terms of a different assignment, however, weeks before the revision, Rick worked by association, not requirement, into a discussion of his essay's unquestioned assumption. For reasons we will explore shortly, he was able to consider in a new context what he could not in the old—that there *might be* a reason for the ridiculous speed. Seeing the authoritative assumptions of "The Experience" as family relationships in "Childhood Entitlements," Rick was able to follow his associations and to interanimate disparate experiences for a new understanding of his race to Cape Cod. In "Childhood Entitlements," we can see the critical effects of a dialogue with authoritative discourse, effects that are largely suppressed in the papers that both precede and follow it. To understand the significance of these critical effects, however, we must first look at one more section of Rick's essay, "The Experience."

In that essay, Rick presents the perspectives of the people in the other two cars in addition to his own: "They were practically yelling at me because they said what I did was extremely dangerous. I tried to explain to them that it wasn't as if I planned it, but they just kept screaming." It may be difficult to understand the descriptive equivalence here between friends who were "practically yelling" and friends who "just kept screaming." Similarly, it may be difficult to understand why Rick would characterize his friends' version of what he had done by the phrase "extremely dangerous." Substituting the didactic discourse of a parent to a child for his friends' speech to him, he seems to be containing the scene with "proper" language that will conform to an adult reader's values. This is not a surprise. It is consistent with other instances of Rick preempting further thought with an oddly placed adult rejoinder. The surprise lies in the particular language for adult authority which he has chosen. He does not say "terribly dangerous" or "very serious" or some such. He contains the judgment of his friends against him with the phrase "extremely dangerous."

In "Childhood Entitlements," Rick's paper on Robert Coles's essay, "Entitlements" (in Bartholomae and Petrosky, 1987), the word "extreme" becomes central. Rick writes that his family's "extreme overprotectiveness" had been handed down to him as his legacy or entitlement. This legacy had multiple, even contradictory effects, sharing only "extreme behavior" in common as he describes in the following excerpt:

> When I was a child I was raised with values very similar with those that my friends were raised with. The one very noticeable difference (even at a young age) was the extreme overprotectiveness that my parents had for me. I wouldn't be allowed to go outside and play with my friends if it was after a certain time in the evening. One of the few things that I was allowed to take part in were local sports clubs. The most memorable of these clubs was a local basketball team that I was on. The overprotectiveness showed through in this aspect of my life as well as others. While my friends on the team were allowed to meet each other before the games and practices, I had to wait for my mother to give me a ride to the gym where these events were held. In my mother's defense I would have to say that the gym was in a rather rough neighborhood that was known for its illegal activities. But there hadn't been any incidents with the other kids on the team and I felt left out for not being able to walk with them.
>
> This overprotectiveness, as I have noticed in the past few years, is becoming increasingly more evident in my own behavior. A prime example of this was when one of my younger sisters was being teased by an older kid in the neighborhood. All I can remember is that she came in the house screaming and crying about what had happened. Right after I heard the story I ran outside, went up to the kid, spit in his face, and ran back to the house as fast as I could. After about a block the kid caught up with me and hit me a few times. But the point I am trying to make is that the overprotectiveness that my parents have for me is becoming a noticeable characteristic of my behavior. Some people might just

view this incident as me trying to protect one of my sisters when they were in trouble. However, I have noticed that rather than just acting normally about something, I tend to go overboard. Rather than just going up to the kid and asking him to stop, I just lost it. Another example (not of overprotectiveness but of extreme behavior) would be the trip to Cape Cod. I was willing to risk everything just to win a race that meant nothing to anyone (not including bragging rights). This could be that since I was so overprotected, whenever I get the chance I go to the farthest extreme I can.

It is impossible to say with certainty that the didactic phrase "extremely dangerous" is the negative marker of Rick's suppressed dialogue with himself about going to extremes in the race to Cape Cod. But it is not necessary to possess certainty. Whether as example or metaphor, we can still observe that the dialogic imagination is capable of very different actions on similar materials in different contexts. Possibly one can go further than this by making some distinctions between those contexts that permit dialogization and those that do not.

As we have seen, in "The Experience" Rick invokes authoritative judgment sheerly as dictum, as rule of thumb: "There wasn't any reason for any ridiculous speed." Whatever understanding he might already have that his family history has contributed to his extreme need to win the race will not stand up to this preemptive authoritative language, language that is dissociated from all circumstance: "The authoritative word," Bakhtin writes, "is located in a distanced zone, organically connected with a past that is felt to be hierarchically higher" (342). Although Rick may know other things about himself, he cannot speak back directly to these dicta. Through a number of containment strategies that draw attention to themselves, we have seen how he fends off dialogue *as* his fórm of dialogue. No revision of this material, it would seem, could position Rick to speak back and say, "There was a reason for the ridiculous speed."

Yet, after reading and writing about two essays in which childhood experiences are associated with specific adult behaviors and values, Rick may be finding authoritative confirmation for what have heretofore been vague, private hunches—"backed by no authority at all" (342). Through the double actions of writing about these essays and relating them to his own experiences, various forms of assimilation begin to occur, ranging from negative and authority-bound to surprisingly dynamic and internally persuasive juxtapositions of disparate experiences, which ultimately constitute a rejoinder to the statement: "There wasn't any reason for any ridiculous speed."

Supported by the idea that one has entitlements or legacies, Rick is able to associate his own overprotection of his sister with his race to Cape Cod, finding in both evidence of his extreme overprotection as a child. Looking at his values historically, he is released, to a certain extent, from a narrative form that has only given him access to these values as "generally acknowledged truths," truths to be accepted or rejected—not discussed (344). By studying his entitlements, he finds he can associate from experience to experience, recontextualize old material and begin to answer it back.

Associating, recontextualizing, and answering back are methods for opening up one's discourse to critical, internally persuasive relations; they are not discrete, cognitive functions that could effectively be taught as techniques apart from one's history of dialogic struggle. If used systematically, for instance, to replace the classical modes of rhetoric, such methods would quickly reproduce the old problems of authoritative pedagogies in general. In a distinction that is difficult to make, we must try to see these methods not as techniques but as actions that can be taken in relation to specific socio-ideological contexts in which students write and think and live their lives. In the case of Rick, they are actions in language that can be differentiated from the other actions he takes—such as going to extremes with his pseudo-objective narration of the race to the Cape. Going "overboard" in his naive self-presentation, Rick listened to many students speak back to his anonymous text, questioning his "amazement" at his friends' anger, doubting his sobriety at the time of the race. Having gone to extremes again, this time in freshman English, Rick reorients himself to the "Entitlements" assignment in a way that allows "newer ways to mean" via association, recontextualization, and retort (Bakhtin, 1981: 346). One can conjecture that something about the repetition of "going overboard" in the context of his college writing disturbed him, put him into struggle, as Bakhtin writes, "for hegemony among various available verbal and ideological points of view, approaches, directions and values" that were becoming available to him (346).

In short, his writing became a site of struggle with his entitlement, not a memoir of struggles elsewhere. Thus, his compositions are characterized by approach *and* retreat, both a selective *and* wholesale assimilation of others' words, both a playing with discourse boundaries *and* and a guarding of them. This unevenness, as we have seen, manifests itself from paper to paper as well as within single papers. One final example will suffice.

Following his discussion in "Childhood Entitlements" of his tendency to go to extremes, Rick returns to a discussion of Coles's essay, writing that it supports the idea "that the style of upbringing and your parents' attitudes are almost always passed down to their children." Having connected his overprotection of his sister with his race to Cape Cod, he extends his thoughts about parent–child relations back to Coles's essay:

> [A]s of late I have noticed myself having many of the same habits and ideals as those of my parents. These similar attributes between parents and their children are most noticeable in the Coles study of the girl who lived just outside of Boston. Her attitude was almost identical with that of her mothers'. While seeing Santa Claus on a visit to Boston she noticed that all the boys were given plastic squirt guns, and the girls were given dolls. After seeing this the girl asked her mother, "why kids wanted to push each other, just to get that junk" (105). Her mother replied, "a lot of people just don't know any better" (105). Rather than her mother saying that either they couldn't afford anything better or that it was a great experience for the children to see Santa Claus, she replied with the same ignorance her daughter was guilty of.

In an interesting turn on the prior essay, Rick speaks back to the language of parental authority. Questioning the mother's values, he is dialogically engaged in a critique of her point of view, going so far as to offer alternatives such as, "they couldn't afford anything better or that it was a great experience for the children to see Santa Claus." Taken together with the opening section of the essay where he criticizes his own mother's overprotectiveness and finds in it some "reason" for his speeding, we have an essay demonstrating critical play with others' words as points of view. Given the active nature of his relativizing consciouness in this essay, it is not surprising that in the conclusion he retreats from the response-ability he has shown. Writing of the mother and daughter in the Coles' essay, he concludes:

> It is probably safe to say that this attitude will remain constant for generations in her family being passed down from a mother to her daughter. This could also be said for almost every household in the country. Each generation will show some remnants of the one before them, so it is up to the parents to educate their children on subjects that they feel they hadn't been "entitled" to be taught about.

Logically, it would not be possible for parents to educate their children to a new understanding they do not possess. The only way the final sentence makes sense is if the positions of parents and children are reversed: "so it is up to the children to educate their parents on subjects they feel they hadn't been 'entitled' to be taught about." Having begun to forge his own discourse relations out of the various discourses he has access to, Rick, it would seem, has something new to tell his parents, to "teach" them—but for him, such a subject position still contradicts his dominant beliefs. Thus, he reverses the agents of knowledge in his final sentence. If what we have seen so far represents any sort of pattern, we might be able to predict that it is precisely these kinds of logical jams and semantic reversals that will continue to make Rick's life as a student difficult for him in a familiar, historically immediate way. For this very reason, he has cause to struggle dialogically toward "newer ways to mean"—not ultimately because of course requirements but because saying less than he knows, or reversing what he knows or exaggerating what he knows at the expense of syntax and logic, constitutes his history in action and leads, one way or another, to further action. The function of a dialogic course sequence is to broaden his range of responses to his history along with his understanding of their implications for his developing subjectivity.

FOUR

Working the Relations between Academic Discourse and Subjectivity: A Cautionary Tale

> Through dialogue, the teacher-of-the-student and the-student-of-the-teacher cease to exist and a new term emerges: teacher–student with student–teachers. The teacher is no longer merely the-one-who-teaches, but one who is himself taught in dialogue with the students, who in turn while being taught also teach. They become jointly responsible for a process in which all grow.
>
> —Paulo Freire, *Pedagogy of the Oppressed*, 67

I

In light of various Marxist and poststuctéuralist theories of knowledge, composition scholars have become increasingly reflective about teacher–student relations. There is considerable concern that poststructural pedagogies, based as they are on a critique of Western idealism, are nevertheless reverting, under institutional pressure, to traditional relations with their materials and their students. Observing this contradiction, Kurt Spellmeyer has written, "[M]any poststructuralist teachers claim to reveal the deep truth, not only about knowledge but also about the knower—a claim no more consistent with any genuine collectivity than with poststructuralism as a discourse that has avowedly abandoned the pursuit of 'truth' itself" (1993: 239).

Implicit in such a critique is a challenge to composition teachers to continue rethinking their pedagogical relations in the fundamental ways articulated by Paulo Freire above. In fact, composition scholarship offers powerful examples of teachers who have responded to the challenge represented by Freire's statement and have struggled toward teacher–student status in their work. When, for instance, Spellmeyer redefines the "common ground" between teachers and students not as their identical perspectives but as their joint capacity for dialogue, he implies radically different relations between teachers and students than is common to education in general or to composition in particular. Working from the assumption that "the dissenting voice never fails to speak truthfully about its situation," Spellmeyer contends that such a voice "may show us all the way to a more encompassing view of our collective reality" (253). Toward the elaboration of their dissenting views, Spellmeyer encourages his students with questions. Rather than a teacher–student, however, he defines his role as the maieutic dialectician, the midwife, "who does not pretend to know what must happen in the practice of questioning, but patiently, carefully prepares the way for an insight that will come on its own terms, in its own time" (255).

As an alternative to the role of the master teacher, this role of midwife (as my work with Rick L. would confirm) is tremendously important, but it does not go far enough. Its differences with the Freireian concept of the teacher–student show up as its own internal contradictions. Because these contradictions are indicative of larger struggles in the field, I will pursue their analysis at some length.

The maieutic dialectician is seemingly neutral: he "does not pretend to know what will happen in the practice of questioning." Still, questions must be formed on some basis. For Spellmeyer, as for Freire, the basis for these questions rests in a commitment to struggle against domination through their educational practices. With domination built into the educational apparatus as it is, Spellmeyer (242) asks, "How can we implement an emancipatory pedagogy that does not entail the manipulation of its 'subjects'?" As an answer, taking the role of the neutral, patient questioner is somewhat insufficient, if not contradictory. After all, every question asked of a student will, in some way, be informed by these commitments to what Spellmeyer himself calls a "specific account of knowledge and a specific vision of social existence" (255).

Maieutic patience, separated from the study of this particular "account of knowledge," this "vision of social existence," and its differences with other accounts, other visions, comes perilously close to a new dialogic formalism. It departs significantly from Freire's project, which takes students and teachers beyond a voicing of their diverse views to an analysis of the social functions of these views. The student who does not know what account of knowledge and vision of existence her patient teacher's questions are part of may ultimately experience her "labor" as an end in itself—something no real midwife would ever find very helpful to the delivery process.

To be sure, Spellmeyer's discussion of the maieutic dialectician is sensitively articulated and convincingly contrasted with the "utter futility of knowledge which demands an act of violence against the knower" (256). But between a pluralistic elaboration of local differences and an assaultive presentation of history's treatment of difference lies work for teachers and students to do together. Freire argues that this work does not inevitably lead to dominating students with the problems of domination, but activates dialectical thinking which is itself the method for analyzing these problems. Dialectical thinking is the process by which one investigates the relations between an individual or group inequity (contradiction) and its larger social function. It demythologizes the explanations that have served to naturalize these inequities. It is a method for determining the specific effects of power relations on knowledge and subjectivity, effects deeply relevant to a critical education in reading and writing.

In this vein, Spellmeyer does work to balance his discussion of the teacher as maieutic dialectician with a discussion of the student as dialectician. It is the essay form itself, he argues, that comes closest to generically representing dialectical thought. For this reason, Spellmeyer defends teaching the essay in freshman English despite its general absence across the curriculum. As conceived by Montaigne, the essay is characterized by personal acts of reflection on one's experiences and presuppositions, whereas current discipline-specific writing in the academy is characterized by their suppression. Teaching the essay, he argues, will initiate more critical relations with those other discipline-specific academic discourses by allowing students to challenge their objective, authoritative presumptions while challenging students' notions that objectivity in those subject areas can be achieved without reflection on their *own* presuppositions (112). With this contrast, Spellmeyer casts the essay as the nonfiction prose equivalent of the novel for Bakhtin—both representing dialogic forms, par excellence. He writes, "Disallowing the pose of objectivity through which experts maintain their privileged status as 'knowers,' the essay dramatizes a process of negotiation and revaluation concealed by other genres, a process never wholly methodical or disinterested" (101).

In a critical response to an earlier version of this material, Susan Miller objects to the way Spellmeyer identifies the history of the essay largely with the history of Montaigne's work, and to the way that Montaigne's work itself is presented as completely open and undisguised self-revelation. Reviewing a range of uses to which the essay has been put since Montaigne—including the weeding out of undesirable students at Harvard in the late nineteenth century— Miller argues that students who do not learn about the contradictory history of the essay form itself are no more likely to become critically situated than students in the writing-across-the-curriculum classes Spellmeyer criticizes. Miller writes:

> [R]equiring contemporary students to write essays without explaining this [genre's] textual and institutional past, without explaining what has counted as rhetorical success or failure in this genre, and without explaining the particular culture and economic situations of those in the canon of essayists . . . will continue to embed our students, if inadvertently, in the pedagogic model of failed authorship that first characterized freshman English. I cannot, that is, attach the essay . . . to "autonomous" thought by students who already are embedded in the actuality of "our world," the institution of freshman English. (1990, 333)

For all its trenchancy, Miller's comment nevertheless stands out as unresolved itself. For instance, nowhere does Miller wonder what all the "explaining" she calls for might yield, given the history of "the institution of freshman English." And although she dissents from what she calls Spellmeyer's romanticization of the essay form, saying its teaching will engage students in sincere conversations "about nothing in particular," she has little to say about how students may develop internally persuasive relations with the knowledge "that a genre's historic textual constraints . . . paint boundaries around success and failure" (333).

In short, where Miller is quick to point out the weaknesses in Spellmeyer's overemphasis on personal experiences and presuppositions as sources of dialogue about their situatedness, she is slow to recognize that her own discussion overemphasizes genre-based presuppositions as sources of such dialogue. Among the problems with this emphasis is that it ignores how poorly positioned most North American students are for experiencing historical information as more than "nothing in particular." Still, in calling Spellmeyer to task for not including the essay itself as a discipline-specific form with its own mixed history, Miller correctly adds a layer of determination to the conversation about situated knowledge that essay writing in freshman English makes possible.

The question of how students may develop internally persuasive discourse relations with this layer of determination remains unanswered, however. This chapter explores some of the possibilities and problems related to this question. To begin, it would seem that Spellmeyer's analysis of the essay form as decisively dialogical points the way to an answer. By exploring the relations between the personal and the social, essay writing invites students to recontextualize their experience by bringing it into contact with authoritative languages that they may struggle with and against. These efforts to forge internally persuasive relations may begin with a single set of determinations, as, for example, Spellmeyer's intentionally modest sample essay: Sartre and the death of a pet. Such essays may create the possibility for entertaining further determinations, including the essay form's "historic textual constraints" (333). However, prematurely requiring this level of determination will certainly lead many students to write recitatively. In short, the concept of overdetermination, which Miller correctly espouses, nevertheless presumes the concept of determination, which the essay form's dialectic between the social and personal may inspire in the way Spellmeyer describes. This is not to argue for a new process pedagogy proceeding from simple to complex determination, but rather to argue against a pedagogy of "correctness" where all the determinations must be in place for any to matter.

The concept of critical effectivity developed in Chapter 2 should remind us that knowledge of one's relationship to any discourse—including the freshman essay—cannot be learned in the fixed manner of a history lesson. In her response to Spellmeyer, Miller tends to idealize the meaning that "a genre's textual constraints" will have for students, treating it as unitary. However, in her elaboration of a textual rhetoric in *Rescuing the Subject*, she does not. If we hold to our notion of the historical subject who is critical in his or her effects, we will see that the study of a genre's history will produce knowledge contingent on the materials that students name as having been constrained and the weight this may carry for them at the time. Critical understanding of the essay form's ideological effects cannot be achieved all at once or once and for all. Subject to ongoing determinations, the ideological effects of a genre on a writer will always be eminently specific, and the meaning that these effects have for students will often be ambiguous.

Furthermore, despite the recognitions that students may achieve by studying a genre's history, the omission of such study does not (as Miller implies) relegate an essay to isomorphic status. In Chapter 2, we looked at a student's essay about her mother's emigration. As she analyzes the history and politics of the event's representation in the media, the author begins to reflect on her representative practices. Noticing her own processes of selecting and prioritizing, she begins to see in her version of her mother's emigration not the true story, but, rather, a "contrary image," one that her relationship to the material calls for in the present. Her essay writing in the present becomes a rejoinder to the authoritative discourses dominating her mother's past and to some extent her own. In her work, she struggles to resist the traditional role of the writing student as neutral recorder of conflicts elsewhere—without having studied this tradition directly. What she has studied directly, through Berger, is dialectical thinking and cultural hegemony. Her self-consciousness about essay writing emerges from this study in relation to media representations of her mother's emigration.

In the work of another student, Susan M., we will see that much less is understood about the hegemonic discourse effects of college writing, even though the author had studied these effects directly through two chapters of Richard Ohmann's book, *English in America* (1976).[1] In "Freshman English and Administered Thought," Ohmann critically surveys a range of freshman English texts, condemning their skills-based, ahistorical assumptions about the way composers choose subjects, form arguments, and solve problems. When writing is presented largely as a problem of "filling up a subject of pre-established dimensions," he argues, it is reduced to a product called "the theme." Theme writing, Ohmann attempts to show in the following chapter, "Writing, Out in the World," is also evident in the rhetorical strategies of powerful institutions beyond the academy. With these institutions emphasizing "problem solving ... abstraction away from historical circumstance, disappearance of the writer as a being with social attributes, and denial of politics," Ohmann finds that the theme writing he objects to in freshman English constitutes successful writing elsewhere (206). In short, theme writing has a conservative social function that makes it useful, if not critical.

When students in composition read Ohmann's analysis of writing textbooks, a light is shone on their writing histories, situating these histories in a network of hegemonic relations. In this context, students may be asked to choose a college paper they have written and to interpret it with and against the grain of Ohmann's work. In other words, they may be asked to construct an overdetermined reading of their own college writing. Susan M.'s paper, "Interesting Topics," can serve to remind us of the capacity students have to reproduce in the present the very theme writing they would claim to see through. In the example discussed below, Susan's understanding of the theme's textual constraints has done little to affect her reproduction of those constraints.

In "Interesting Topics," she describes a "meaningless" American Studies paper she wrote about gravestones and vernacular architecture for which she received a B grade. Professing no interest in the subject, she claims to find an ally in Ohmann when he warns, "Never write about a topic that you do not believe is worth discussing" (148). Differentiating her present practice from her past, Susan writes:

> During my high school years and through some of my early years at college, I never followed or was never allowed to

follow Ohmann's method of writing. These years were overflowing with occasions for theme writing that involved minimal thinking and idea forming on my part. Teachers and professor would dictat "Write about anything you want to write about, but make sure that you choose from this list of themes and topics that I have given you." What about the student who is not interested in anything that is on the list? What happens to her? My paper is a prime example of a writer who is not interested in the topic of her paper.

Vernacular architecture or folk buildings are built without formal plans and are usually constructed by the owner. Vernacular architecture is bilateral and tripartite . . .

Again, where is my opinion? I struggled with this paper for some time but it still turned out to be a theme paper. Why not? The only type of papers that I knew how to write at this time were theme papers, This topic does not connect with any of my interests or experiences. I am not saying that every subject that a person writes about is earth shattering to them, but every time I was given one of these assignments, it was about the teacher's topic. Everything I wrote about had to interest the teacher. It made no difference if the topic interested me.

It will not be an irony lost on the reader that the topic of vernacular architecture, as evident in the citation above, potentially contains much that the author might find relevant now: constructions built by owners, "without formal plans," to fit their needs and interests would seem to be a metaphor for the kind of writing the author wishes to do. However, Susan virtually explains to us why noticing such an affinity in the present is not possible: her subjectivity as a student is defined as a receiver's subjectivity—someone who is dictated to. Her response to the present assignment has not been altered by Ohmann's historical confirmation that she has indeed been constructed to receive and assemble preformed materials. Rather, in this paper, she dutifully receives and assembles Ohmann's work in relation to her own. She also applies the assumption underpinning that work: that no one could read such a text and remain unchanged. Thus, she posits change in the familiar before/after rhetoric of freshman writing, a rhetoric about which she is no more aware than she is aware of the wish-fulfillment represented by the example she has chosen of vernacular architecture.

In short, the assumption that historical knowledge of academic forms will alter one's subjectivity and affect one's present situation is an idealism and must be rethought. Tending toward reification in pedagogical contexts, the concept of historicity easily threatens to become the key concept of a new, authoritative discourse—the chief evidence of which is student mimicry.

In the paragraph that follows the one by Susan cited above, she is again helpful in explaining why a reading of Ohmann might not affect her theme writing in the present. "For me," she writes in regard to her architecture paper, "the subject only had a 'book life' . . . I did not really understand what I was working with or working for." Subject to the book *still*, she quickly transforms Ohmann's analysis of this hegemonic relation into its repetition. By contrast, the author of the essay on her mother's emigration finds a context in which a struggle with her relations to media representations can take place. One cannot, it would seem, make any simple assumptions about which historical materials might promote reflection about one's subject position, this matter of subjectivity being the central one.

In other words, it is a mistake of ahistorical thinking to presume that reflection on the essay form's constraints will *always* produce more awareness of one's situated knowledge and subjectivity than other kinds of reflections as the contrast between the two writers above suggests. Indeed, the absoluteness with which Miller pursues a distinction between her project and Spellmeyer's ultimately suggests indifference to the overdetermined nature of student subjectivity and thus—recalling Freire's teacher–student—the overdetermined nature of pedagogical responses to it. This said, there is nevertheless much to explore in the proposal that critical reflection on one's situation should include one's situation as a writer in "'our world,' the institution of freshman English" (333).

II

In Chapter 3, we considered Bakhtin's philosophy of language through a graphic model of dialogic relations. In this model, an individual forms horizontal relations with others, including others' discourses, while simultaneously forming vertical relationships between these experiences and one's self. The purpose of this admittedly limited model is to define the individual psyche as always also a social psyche (Emerson, 1983: 249). If we agree to frame the formation of consciousness in terms of these double activities of dialogue with others and dialogue with self about these others, we can see, without too much trouble, why privileging one axis over another would be a pedagogical mistake. In the case of Susan M. above, one could argue that the horizontal axis (dialogue with Ohmann about freshman English discourse) is insufficiently submitted to vertical consideration. As such, her relation to "the book" remains largely authoritative, which is to say untransformed by internally persuasive dialogue with it. It may be that in her striking metaphor of "book life," Susan shows herself to be in an early stage of struggle for a different subject position and that this critical representation could be taken further through teacher–student dialogue. My purpose, however, is not to discuss a pedagogy for Susan but to put the issue of examining one's relations to college essay writing into the context of Bakhtin's dialogic model of consciousness.

It is one thing, as we have seen, to learn about our overdetermined discourse relations (for instance, that the freshman English theme is not a neutral or timeless form). It is another thing, as we have also seen, to make something of this knowledge which will bear on one's relation to it. Although Miller emphasizes the importance of the first aspect, I would argue that we must include both. It is the *double activities* of "learning about" and "making something of" that structure consciousness as an act of becoming. As double activities, they must be kept up. In other words, critical consciousness or consciousness of one's historicity must be approached as an activity involving both study of particular determinations and play with the notion of determination itself toward internally persuasive relations with it. The two activities may be complementary, but they are not always so: a particular determination under study may be subject to negative dialogics and not engage much play, as the example of Susan M. suggests. A dialogic sequence should be capable of responding to this difficulty, shifting to a level of determination that gives the significance of such dialectical thinking a chance of finding some internally persuasive form. Only our residual positivism, wedded to the concept of determination, could create this odd-seeming but nevertheless commonly felt contradiction between the dialogic imagination and dialectical thinking.

Thus, although students should be given opportunities to historicize the discourse relations they are in, it should be emphasized that this activity comes with no guarantees—it is not an end in itself. However, as part of a larger set of double activities by which students learn about and make something of their subject relations, the analysis of academic discourses can be significant. Students of composition can learn to analyze the historical contexts that motivate and sustain their relations to composition and other academic discourses, using this knowledge toward the evolution of a critical style that does not depend on any one of these academic languages to fix their voices or limit their perspectives. Extending Bakhtin's concept of internally persuasive discourse relations to the academy, one can argue that as students learn to historicize the discourse relations they are in, they are being given at the same time the means to forge a university discourse that has not yet been written but that, upon its materialization, becomes part of the university-in-process. What we can expect such writing to look like, how we will know it when we see it, and how we can respond to it are questions I will continue to address.

III

Before proceeding further, it is important to review why we would try to approach the teaching of reading and writing in this reflexive, historical way. That we can is one thing; that we would choose to, however, is another. We would, after all, be teaching our students to read academic discourses ideologically, that is, as structures of representation, and to discover how their own subjectivity is affected by these academic forms of representation.

The alternative to teaching our students to read these discourses ideologically is not, as one might wish, a simpler or less ideological approach; it is simply less visibly ideological. When students, as in many writing across the curriculum programs, are taught various academic discourses in the name of a neutral pluralism, they are being offered a consumer ideology. This ideology represents the student as an individual free to choose among various brand-name discourses in the marketplace of ideas. This representation of forms of knowledge as equal competitors suppresses the role that history and power have played in the emergence of certain fields as fields. It suppresses, as well, the role history and power have played in forming a view of students as free to choose among neutral languages toward the acquisition of knowledge.

As in the teaching of writing across the curriculum, so, too, in the teaching of writing *within* English departments, we can find specific assumptions about language and self that structure our courses and our responses to our students in those courses. In his article, "Judging Writing, Judging Selves," Lester Faigley (1989) goes to some length to analyze the unstated values and belief systems composing the criteria for good college writing by two generations of writing instructors in 1931 and 1985.[2] As different as the written products would appear to be between the 1931 and 1985 pool of students that he researches, Faigley shows how an assumption about language originating within the minds of individuals lies behind each. In the 1931 case, the winning discourse expressed, for the academic readers evaluating it, a "natural" tastefulness and sensitivity originating wholly in the minds of particularly able students (402). In the 1985 case, those essays that appear to be the most revealing of a true self are commended by their readers for achieving this effect by constructing a true language about the writers' "selves" (405).

In short, the philosophical ideal of a true and unified self that is expressible through the transparent medium of language has had its place within English departments, influencing what students write and what teachers value. One effect has been the valorization of a particular undergraduate English composition discourse: the before-and-after personal narrative. Faigley writes, "The student selves that we encounter... are predominantly selves that achieve rationality and unity by characterizing former selves as objects for analysis, hence the emphasis on writing about past experience rather than confronting the contradictions of present experience" (411).

This other option, that is, "confronting the contradictions of present experience," has the potential for eliciting more analysis of and greater directness about the discourses that structure our ways of knowing and using language in the university. Faigley's example of such a "confrontation," however, is somewhat puzzling. Working with the final three paragraphs of the "best" essay ever received by William E. Coles, Faigley differentiates it from other examples of student writing he has cited by saying, "Unlike most of the other[s] . . . it does not present a unified subject position nor does it finally decide on a single metaphor for the university. The student writer . . . weaves together several conflicting discourses and images that college students experience without attempting to resolve the conflicts" (409). Here is the passage from the essay to which he is referring:

> I used to have conversations about D. H. Lawrence with a friend in the elevator. It started one day when I noticed a copy of *The Rainbow* under his arm, and he noticed a copy under mine. The conversations did not last long—just long enough for the elevator to get from the 6th floor to the lobby, but now the only time I see my friend is in a class we have together. We say hello, but that is all we say.
> My wife has started to read Lawrence, though, and I talk with her about him.
> Sometimes in our apartment we're conscious of the Rapid going by; sometimes we're not. (409)

Faigley seems to offer this example as a critical alternative to student writing, which proceeds from assumptions about the self as rational and unified and from language as expressive of such a self. As a contrast, however, it is only the opposite self of the same discourse: the fragmented, alienated, antirational self. There is no indication that the student writer, George Humphrey, has learned to problematize his discourse and thereby come to some historical understanding of the relationship between the voice of idealism he rejects and the voice of alienation he embraces. As a narrative of loss, it could be argued, the student's essay enacts expressivist and realist assumptions regarding the ability of language to faithfully transcribe emotional reality, in this case, the emotional reality of lost wholeness. Indeed, one could argue that the humanist tradition has been spectacularly successful at reproducing itself precisely because it has normalized as a subgenre this literature of loss, of disenchantment. Thus, in short, the vast mimetic literature of lost wholeness (including the essay by student George Humphrey) projects contradiction fatalistically, historicizing neither the sources of the fatalism nor its social function.

Having inscribed himself in this tradition so concretely, however, the writer of the essay is certainly in a position to look again at his writing, to see its language "through the eyes of another language" (Bakhtin, 1981: 296). By so doing, the fragmented experience of university discourse relations could lose some of its mystification, and the presupposition that lost wholeness motivates a radically new student discourse could be examined. The student could begin to find some historical logic in the contradictions he has perceived and even some new sense of himself as student, neither nostalgic for lost unity nor resigned to senseless contradiction—as the humanist framework would have it—but rather, dialogically engaged in an examination of these perspectives and their impact on his relationship to his schooling. Indeed, this is the project Faigley envisions when he states that writing teachers can teach students "to analyze cultural definitions of the self, to understand how historically these definitions are created in discourse and to recognize how definitions of the self are involved in the configuration of relations of power" (411).

It remains the purpose of this chapter to draw out the implications of the above discussion by shifting to another sample of student writing which also tries to confront "the contradictions of present experience" in an academic setting. As historicizing educators, we may choose to problematize academic discourse. In this way, we invite students into the contradictions of their present setting, and we submit the idealisms by which such contradictions are contained to dialectical review. Under those circumstances, both cultural definitions of the self and the discourses that construct them (including university discourses) play a role in the consideration of our social consciousness along what we are calling Bakhtin's horizontal axis. In addition to this horizontal axis, we must include the vertical, where a struggle for internally persuasive, transformative relations *with* these determinations needs to take place. In the context of such double action, we may find that something learned about the discourse relations of the university becomes something learned about one's own composition by discourse.

IV

The following student paper is by Michelle Y., a Hong Kong emigré from the management school, enrolled in an advanced composition course. In this paper, it is possible to see what the writer learns (and doesn't learn) about the structuring effects of discourse as she studies the university discourse relations she is in. As with Susan M.'s assignment, this one invited advanced composition students to interpret an artifact of their own schooling in relation to two chapters from Richard Ohmann's book, *English in America*: "Freshman English and Administered Thought" and "Writing, Out in the World." This assignment (#7) was part of the sequence outlined in Chapter 2. The students began with a reading of *About Looking* where they worked with the history of men's suits as an example of cultural hegemony and continued in this vein with work on the uses of photography. In her response to Assignment 7, Michelle focuses on a professional course she is taking, Theory and Practice of Management, putting it into dialogue with three readings: Ohmann's text (from the present course); Walker Percy's "The Loss of the Creature" (from a prior course); and Jonathon Kozol's article, "The Homeless and Their Children." The last, a two-part excerpt from *Rachel's Children*, became available to her when she requested suggestions for "outside reading." Seen as emerging critique, Michelle's essay represents an alternative to the discourse of writing across the curriculum where a neutral pluralism often substitutes for the critical interanimation of academic languages and points of view. Her essay, somewhat shortened, reads as follows:

> After reading Ohmann's "Freshman Composition and Administered Thought" and "Writing Out in the World," I sort of heard what he says about the dangerous effects of some systematical writing teaching methods in this country on the thinking and planning process of college students, who will be the planners of the future (173). He contests the cookbook method of teaching college students how to write. Choosing

a subject, classification, and tone—all these, to Ohmann, are to pre-establish dimensions of a writing subject hence limiting the writer's thought. Nontheless, those modes of writing that Ohmann refutes were undoubtedly accepted by me during these years of college education. They became my panacea. Therefore, although I heard Ohmann's argument, it seemed to me so remote from my understanding. In fact, the other day in class, I expressed my acceptance of the mode of business writing and criticized Ohmann being unable to see things from other perspectives such as that of a business person.

Due to my problem with Ohmann's argument, I had a hard time at the beginning trying to fulfill Assignment 7. Instead of merely finding something to write about, I decided to put it off for a couple of days and let my thoughts come naturally. In the meantime, I had read the article of Jonathon Kozol, "The Homeless" in *The New Yorker*. Neither did the statistics nor the condition of the homeless people reported by Kozol strike me but the way he saw the homeless did. Family breakdown, drugs, a culture of poverty, teenage pregnancies, the underclass—to Kozol, none of these familiar explanations are the cause of homelessness but the lack of affordable housing is; therefore the blame is not on the homeless people but on society, which is composed of political, economic and personal factors. However, I failed to see it and my initial response to those homeless mothers whom I saw on TV was apathetic, if not antipathetic: "If you [those homeless women] can't afford to have a child, don't have sex." They offended me because "they take some of our taxes for their food, their clothing, their hurried clinic visits and their shelter." Considering those homeless people as a liability, not an asset, to society, I was using the cost-benefit analysis method, which I learned in my management class, to evaluate their value to society. Their being was therefore reduced to an abstract figure in a cost-benefit equation. My perception of those homeless mothers shocked my conscience when I compared my perception with Kozol's. Therefore, I must re-examine my management 301 course.

I will first look at the text book for the course, then the course assignments. The main theme of the text (other management books as well) is the four functions of management: planning, organizing, leading and controlling, which is a form of problem solving procedures. According to the text, the first and also the most important step of problem solving is to define the problem and set objectives which should be specific and measurable. In order to be specific, thought should be narrowed; in order to be measurable, things must be put in units. . . . The author of the text even lists the steps in problem solving:

1. Finding and defining the problem
2. Generation of alternative solutions
3. Evaluation of alternatives and selection of a preferred solution
4. Implementation of preferred solution
5. Evaluation of results

This problem-solving model appears throughout the text . . . as a magic wand. The student's job is to apply the model to all types of problems. Ohmann, in his essay, pointed out a similar problem-solving formula used by the strategists for the Pentagon Papers which "are variants on a simple form of argument, dictated by the situation" (196). He also says: "any model reduces complexity—exchanges faithfulness to reality for finiteness" and "a problem-solving model supplies a grid that connects reality to a desired future by one or more acts" (196).

In our case study assignment, we used the "Grade and Feedback Form" [below] which was the teacher's pre-determined outline or format for the case . . . :

Grading Areas Points	Maximum
1. Summary of fact	5
2. Statement of problem	15
3. Symptoms	5
4. Causes	15
5. Alternate solutions	20
6. Discussion, solution, justification	<u>40</u>
	100

There are several things in the format that I want to emphasize. First, it is the fragmentation of the paper by the way that the teacher was going to grade it. He assigned certain points to each part of the paper. In an extreme situation, the student who did not state the problem or the causes of the case at all but did well in the other parts of the paper could still get 85 points or a decent B grade. But the paper would not make any meaning. Second, like memo writers of the Pentagon Papers, the student had "limited freedom not only in what he [could] say, but in the form of its saying as well. His writing strategy was pretty well defined by his situation" (195). Lastly, the student's thought was not just confined by the format itself but limited by the grading system. The format set a ceiling to the student's creativity because of the "maximum points" that he or she could achieve. . . . Take myself as an example. When doing that assignment I wanted to come up with only three possible solutions to the case, no more than three as I would not gain any extra credit and it would not do any good to my assignment. Thus, my thought inevitably stopped there.

Now let's turn to the content of my paper. The case was about the departmentalization at Levi Strauss. The company had experienced . . . increased competition from abroad. Low wages paid to apparel workers in other countries offered foreign manufacturers a distinct price advantage. . . . My purpose for writing the paper was to analyze Levi Strauss and Company's present organizational structure and point out its advantages and disadvantages, then I was to suggest changes that should be made to its present organizational structure so as to help it cope with its external environment changes and be successful in the 1990s.

After re-reading my paper, I found that my analysis of the case and my suggested solutions were based only on profit and loss. For example, my prime objective was to cut manufacturing costs, fixed overhead, and even administrative costs, in order to be more competitive in the market place. Although being more creative in designing their products . . . could be a better alternative, cutting costs would be easiest to be measured. However, it inevitably led to closing down unprofitable plants, laying off excessive employees, and replacing workers by robots to increase productivity. Those affected workers were not considered as if they did not exist in the picture. Due to the lay-off, some of the affected workers and their families could become homeless. They could, as Kozol says, lose not only their job and their homes, but also their families. But all these cannot be measured by any simple methods, so their futures, feelings, and families which could not be transformed into figures, were left out from my profit and loss equation.

My decision and suggested solutions to the case study were inhumane but would not hurt any real people. Yet, my inhumanity has been affirmed by the grade, an A, that I got for the paper. If we extend out imagination that I will be a manager or a decision maker (probably I will) in the business world, my decision would have its effect on real people. Try to stretch the imagination a bit more. Nowadays, an MBA degree seems to be the key to a managerial position and this kind of management course is the core course of the program. That means every MBA graduate has taken this kind of management course; his or her thinking process and behavior, like mine, probably has been influenced by the course structure and materials. When these people—MBA graduates—use what they have learned in their management courses without realizing its shortcomings . . . the effect will be enormous. In the textile industry, for example, now, many American manufacturers have their products made in many newly developing countries which have low labor costs. As a result of the shift to overseas manufacturing, the employment in the industry has declined by over 200,000 since 1980. Some of these 200,000 layoffs very likely became frequent residents of homeless hotels and shelters. Some people, like me before, see them as non-productive, a liability to society. Nevertheless, they are forced to be in that situation due to management's decision to cut production costs. Now they are seen as a cost to society. Does it mean that they should also be eliminated from society? Is this why the government does not provide enough low-income housing for these people in order to eliminate them? As Kozol says, after having lived in a shelter or homeless hotel for a period of time, just as the physical condition of those people deteriorates, so too their internal spirit collapses. Although we want to minimize any costs and maximize profits, we do not care to minimize this non-numerical cost of homeless people.

Having reviewed the MGT 301 course and my assignment, I can hardly disagree with Ohmann's argument—student's thinking processes can be influenced by the way they are taught to write and some groups of people are purposely or not purposely trying to use certain modes of writing to maintain the status quo. The blame or the responsibility seems to be merely on educators, text book authors and experts. How about we students? Are we also responsible for passively accepting the confinement? Students (and many people) like formulas, theories and models which are believed to provide security and keys to success. What has taken place is a "loss of sovereignty" from students to experts. Being of "service, docile, and limited," rather than being "free, critical and creative," students lose their freedom to get out of the preestablished boundaries. (142)

Certainly, the writer has achieved a substantial amount of understanding regarding the university discourse relations she is in, as well as her own composition by discourse. Applying Walker Percy's metaphor of the magic wand to the problem-solving model, she discusses how the methods of her management course necessarily lead to certain conclusions and in that way "set ceilings" on creativity. She sees the content of the course ideologically—as the structuring of a point of view—and identifies the structure with the discourse of profit and loss. Going a step further, she approaches what Michel Foucault in *Discipline and Punish* would call the microphysics of this structure. She explains that her solutions for Levi Strauss's problems depend on cost-cutting rather than design innovation because "cutting costs would be the easiest to be measured." Measurability, seen here in a Foucauldian way as a means of normative control, thus supersedes even profitability in this discourse.

By observing what this discourse allows her to see and not see, to feel and not feel, the writer is beginning to notice the influence of discourse on her thinking. Discovering that her cost-cutting solution ignored the workers who would be laid off, she goes on to reflect about the course in general: "[T]his kind of management course is the core of the program... every MBA graduate has taken this kind of course; his or her thinking process, like mine, probably has been influenced by the course structure and materials. When these people—MBA graduates—use what they have learned in their management courses without realizing its shortcomings to make decisions for their companies, for society, the effect will be enormous." The extent to which Michelle has entered into a critique of this discourse and her own composition by it is evident, I think, in what follows. Rather than letting us hang on the idea of "enormous" effects, she goes on to imagine them and by doing so, struggles against the influence of the management discourse's shaping power. Referring to the 200,000 laid-off textile workers in this country, some of whom may have become homeless, she writes, "They are forced to be in that situation due to management's decision. . . . Now they are seen as a cost to society. Is this why the government does not provide enough low-income housing for these people in order to eliminate them?" Michelle may not be the first person to ask this question, but certainly it is new for her to ask it. In this passage, we can see Michelle synthesizing Kozol, Ohmann, and her own research on the textile industry in order to reflect on and extend her own thinking. A discourse of critique is emerging, one that in Mikhail Bakhtin's helpful terms shows signs of becoming internally persuasive and not just authoritative. Although every discourse, Bakhtin argues, is always partly ours and partly others' (345), he goes on to say that the internally persuasive word awakens "new and independent words . . . applied to new material, new conditions; it enters into interanimating relationships with new contexts" (345–46). Imagining the spiritual deterioration of homeless textile workers as a nonnumerical cost and playing this meaning of cost off against its economic meaning, Michelle applies Kozol's and Ohmann's perspectives to the context of the textile industry, thereby illustrating Bakhtin's criteria for an emerging, internally persuasive discourse.

As for what Michelle does not learn about the university discourse relations she is in and her own composition by discourse, there is also much to say. Despite the obvious critical process she is in, Michelle must (as Faigley predicts) turn her story into a before/after narrative of a once-false-and-now-true-self. What we see is how her own continuing composition by an academic-humanist discourse requires her to impose closure via binary oppositions such as before/after; docile/critical; limited/free. At the end, she is still looking for an autonomous position—one that separates her self from her social context—and reestablishes her as the source of her own language, someone who should be able to "get out of" preestablished boundaries individually. This may seem a small point considering all that she has accomplished here, but for this writer, there may be significant consequences for this type of individualistic closure.

In her general references to cheap overseas labor markets undermining Levi Strauss, she avoids a fact that is obvious to anyone familiar with the textile industry: those overseas labor markets are largely in Asia and include her native Hong Kong. Certainly, the writer must experience some conflict when she refers to her homeland as one of those "other countries" that paid "low wages" and thus "offered foreign manufacturers a distinct price advantage." With her family and friends still in Hong Kong, what conflict might she have about who should go unemployed—Americans or Asians? However, she never reaches this point of present contradiction so that she might study these questions. By fundamentally reading the text of her management course from the point of view it assumes—that its readers are white, middle-class American students—she ends up identifying with the hegemonic assumptions that split her student self from aspects of her cultural self. At the end, her expression of personal freedom and responsibility, like the problem-solving model itself, is used as a magic wand to negate aspects of her own social history and the present contradictions that threaten to arise from it. As she cites in Ohmann, so, too, her discourse "reduces complexity" [read social contradiction] and "exchanges faithfulness to reality" [read recognition of her composite self] "for finiteness" [read unity: the white American student for whom the text was composed].

As moving and important as many of her insights are, it is also important to see that, like all of us, Michelle has limits beyond which she simply cannot go right now. "Thus," she writes, "my thought inevitably stopped there." Teachers of writing who seek to develop a pedagogy that investigates the structuring effects of discourse must be careful not to idealize the process and expect new forms of unity and coherence to be produced by the performance of social dialectics. "Our ideological development," Bakhtin writes, ". . . is an intense struggle within us for hegemony among various available verbal and ideological points of view, approaches, directions and values" (345–46).

As writing instructors, we need a concept of contradiction that will help us to accept and accommodate this intense, ongoing struggle toward critical discourse among our students, a struggle that leads them toward both a reproduction of social contradiction and its critique. This struggle with language and ideology is the inevitable effect of historicized discourse relations. However, our acceptance and accommodation, based on a theory of contradiction, are not enough. We must ask ourselves, every step of the way, to what extent we are manipulating the direction of this struggle in the name of ideological development and to what effects.

For instance, it is not accurate to contend that the management discourse alone shapes Michelle's subjectivity in a particular direction. We also need to consider the way that the Ohmann text and the English assignment she is addressing may also influence her identifications with certain points of view and diminish her capacity for dialogic engagement. As we have seen, Michelle writes nothing about the meaning that competition for jobs between the people of her native and adopted countries has for her in the present, despite the evidence in the essay that drawing out this implication is well within her range of concerns. It is not the management discourse alone that limits her thinking about these present contradictions between her student self and cultural self. Ohmann's text as a required course reading is also responsible. Looking back at the first paragraph of Michelle's essay, we can see that she has been insulted by Ohmann's devaluing of the current-traditional rhetoric she has been taught. This rhetoric, which Ohmann describes as a "cookbook" method, she describes as a "panacea." Saying this, she goes about as far as she can in articulating her present differences with Ohmann's point of view. For the rest of the essay, she struggles to bring his "remote" argument closer, and she comes up with an example that is nearly "perfect" in the way it both illustrates Ohmann's thesis and extends it into her own context. Given the elaborateness of her work, it is easy not to notice how Ohmann's insult to her English education affects her work. Only when we draw out the implications of her analysis to the point of present contradictions that she cannot entertain (Who shall go unemployed?) do we get signs of this "perfect" answer's containments and costs. As much as she has learned from this historicizing approach to management discourse, there is also an antihistoricizing force at work. It splits off the student filling this assignment from the second-language student who has found "choosing a subject, classification and tone" significant terms for defining the work of English composition.

Of course, it is not hard to see why she would be confused and insulted by his criticism. There is a virtually perfect match between the methods of the current-traditional rhetoric she refers to as her "panacea" and her management discourse. Indeed, James Berlin, Richard Ohmann, and others offer the thesis that current-traditional rhetoric represents "the triumph of the scientific and technical world view" (Berlin, 1987: 62). With its emphasis on knowledge as a matter of induction and report, current-traditional rhetoric directs its attention to the effective arrangement of one's scientifically derived inductions, a type of attention that Berlin significantly calls "managerial invention." This process places high priority on matters of "subject, classification and tone," particularly as they relate to choices among the modes of discourse (64). Berlin writes:

> The mind is regarded as a set of structures that performs in a rational manner, adjusting and reordering functions in the service of the goal of the individual....
> This entire scheme can be seen as analogous to the instrumental method of the modern corporation.... Their work life is designed to turn goal-seeking and problem-solving behavior into profits. The pursuit of self-evident and unquestioned goals in the composing process parallels the pursuit of self-evident and unquestioned profit-making goals in the corporate marketplace. (1988: 482–83)

Having been so successfully prepared for her management discourse by her English training, Michelle is understandably reluc-

Academic Discourse and Subjectivity   87

tant to criticize an education that has actually been coherent and has seemed to work. Indeed, her invisibility to the authors of her management text would probably seem, from her point of view, much less significant than her invisibility to Ohmann in his text. Despite Ohmann's criticism of composition texts that treat students as lacking social attributes, his writing would seem to have had the effect of negating hers. Unable to articulate this present contradiction between her experience as an ESL student majoring in business and Ohmann's critique of her "panacea," Michelle offers a conversion instead.

Her flawless critique of her business text, by virtue of its flawlessness, suggests itself to be her gifted way of "managing" what for her is a very flawed point of view on Ohmann's part ("The other day in class I expressed my acceptance of the mode of business writing.") Apparently feeling unable to elaborate a rejoinder to Ohmann and feeling debased by the idea that she has valued something deemed to be without value by a course text, she goes on to debase herself in relation to Kozol: "My perception . . . shocked my conscience when I compared . . . [it] with Kozol's." In reaction to such perceived difference and debasement, her strategies are accommodation and simplification. These reactions are evident in the sentence that follows her description of a shocked conscience: "Therefore I must re-examine my management 301 course." Given the rich reexamination that follows, it may seem unreasonable to refer to this sentence in terms of accommodation and simplification. But if we glance back at this section of her essay, we will see that this gateway sentence to the rest of the essay is based on the assertion that the cost-benefit method that she learned in management class is solely responsible for her attitudes toward homeless women, despite the evidence that she brought a prior discourse about women, poverty, and sex to her management class.

This prior discourse about homeless women is given its ideological due by being put in citation: "They offended me," Michelle writes, "because 'they take some of our taxes for their food, their clothing, their hurried clinic visits and their shelter.'" Retrospectively, Michelle notices the similarity between her values and management's and uses a magic wand to confer monologic authority on the discourse favored by the assignment, at the expense of understanding her own heteroglot history on this matter—the way that various available discourses may have mutually supported and structured her subjectivity over time and in different contexts. Conforming herself to a project that she sees as debasing her own writing history, she goes on to reify it. Management discourse becomes the singular cause of values that now shock her as false consciousness and that she works to repudiate. Shutting down dialogue with that part of herself which she sees the assignment debasing, she nevertheless produces significant insights regarding the shaping power of management discourse.

As I have said, in Michelle's writing we are witnessing a hegemonic struggle among discourses and their ideologies, which, as Bakhtin predicts, is "intense" (346). On the one hand, she deconstructs her management discourse. By carefully tracing its effects on her subjectivity, she begins to disidentify with it as a totality. On the other hand, her work is based on the containment of her multilayered subjectivity as the unified effect of her management discourse. Basing it this way, she identifies herself totally with a perspective that erases large areas of her experience. Possibly for the first time, she has been put in the position of naming the discourse relations she is in and, in response, engages with seemingly equal fervor in dialogic inquiry and managerial containment.

Although such gains and losses are an inevitable part of any critical struggle, we must still try to understand them, keeping in mind that pedagogy is a social relationship that cannot be rationalized by accounting approaches to students' texts. Writing astutely about the preoccupation of deconstructionists and other postmodern critics with the analysis of texts, Stanley Aronowitz can help compositionists keep their focus on the relational aspects of these discursive practices for the student. Acknowledging postmodernism's capacity for "dazzling cultural criticism," Aronowitz also notes, "There is little if any sense of pedagogy in this discourse," little if any "understanding of how people invest in signs, signifiers, images and discourses that actively construct their identities and social relations" (72).

In this chapter, I have tried to restore some attention to the way students' investments in their discourses, ideologies, and constructions of self may affect their responses to postmodern pedagogies that problematize these investments in terms of their own writing practices. My purpose has been to ensure that we not mistake a person in the process of ideological becoming with a cultural artifact in the process of deconstruction. Aronowitz's cautionary statement invites us to theorize Michelle's investments in certain "signs, signifiers, images and discourses" even more thoroughly than we yet have.

In his essay, "Border Pedagogy in the Age of Postmodernism," Henry Giroux writes that "students *need to* develop a relationship of non-identity with their own subject positions— through forays across the official borders of knowledge (Aronowitz and Giroux, 1991: 129; emphasis mine). This pedagogy aptly describes the intentions of Michelle's course in advanced composition. Indeed, her relationship to management discourse does appear to have lost some of its neutral authority by virtue of her crossing its key terms with the critical languages of Ohmann and Kozol. However, what educators assert that students "need to develop" may not be identical with students' perceptions of their own needs, and this is where Aronowitz's statement can help. Under these circumstances, as we have seen, students of border pedagogies may be less in the process of establishing a critical relationship of nonidentity with their subject positions and more in the process of prematurely disidentifying with subject positions deemed out of favor. Such appears, at least possibly, to be the case with Michelle. Following Aronowitz, it could be argued that what Michelle "needs to develop" is a more conscious relationship of identity with the subject positions in which she is invested so that an internally persuasive relationship of nonidentity may be established dialectically.

Working with the theories of Hans Georg Gadamer, Greg Spellmeyer (1993) writes persuasively on this point: "Gadamer believes that the learner's presuppositions are the ground from which he or she views the world and that the achievement of understanding requires not the suspension of these presuppositions in some pretended neutrality but a reaffirmation of the self, at first against the question and then within it" (112). Michelle's essay invites us to consider what it might mean for her to study her presuppositions about current-traditional rhetoric in the context of her ESL studies, to work against Ohmann as she is initially inclined in order that she might eventually work within *his* terms less compliantly. It is not hard to imagine that writing about certain academic "panaceas" would put her in a position to write about their uses as well as their limits, less as a convert and more as a student of her own rhetorical history. Premature disidentification with one's subject positions (whatever they are), on the other hand, deprives students of the very contact with their histories that is the basis for understanding the shaping power of their discursive practices.

Thus, it could be said that the route to critical nonidentity with one's investments in certain subject positions cannot be theoretically distinguished from the route to critical identity with those positions, the social nature of subjectivity being central to both. It is at this level of concern for the dialectic of identity/nonidentity with one's subject positions that Freire's notion of the teacher as student most profoundly applies. Michelle's essay invites us to consider what it might mean for the teacher to position herself as the student of the student's dialogical knowledge. Disidentifying with predetermined notions of how a border pedagogy "needs to" proceed, such a teacher would think about how Michelle's investment in her own formation by discourse might become more active and interrogative and less self-abnegating and managerial. In Michelle's case, it would seem that reading against Ohmann might be at least as historicizing of her subjectivity as reading with him has been. Teachers of composition who are working postmodern theory with their students can be influenced by the tendency Aronowitz describes, inadvertently eliciting from their students a display of "dazzling" cultural self-criticism, such as we see in Michelle's work. However incisive and persuasive this work may be, it is still at the expense of dialogue with one's identifications in certain "signs, signifiers, images and discourses" that form, after all, the basis of one's historical self and one's capacity for transformation.

NOTES

1. Ohmann's book addresses many of Miller's requirements. For instance, it investigates freshman English as an institution and the freshman essay as a genre with a history. My use of it as a reference throughout this chapter should be understood in relation to Miller's argument. In other words, I am using it to represent the type of text that historicizes freshman English in the manner Miller describes rather than as the canonical text on the subject. Working with Ohmann's theories in the com-

position classroom thus becomes an instantiation of Miller's textual rhetoric, allowing us to understand and assess some of its effects.

2. A revised version of this essay appears in *Fragments of Rationality: Postmodernity and the Subject of Composition*. I have continued to refer to the first published version of this material because it includes materials relevant to my argument which do not appear in the later version.

FIVE

How-to Hope in Stanley Fish: Foundationalism Reworked

> [Writing practice] has nothing to do with theory, at least in the sense of being enabled and justified by theory. This leaves me and you only a few worn and familiar bromides: practice makes perfect, you learn to write by writing, you must build on what you already know.
> —Stanley Fish, "Anti-foundationalism, Theory Hope and the Teaching of Composition," *Doing What Comes Naturally*, 355

> Composition is ... an existing site for dismantling particularly troublesome versions of hegemonic discursive "common sense"—particularly exclusivity, humiliation, repression, and injustice hidden in the nineteenth-century bourgeois moralities.
> —Susan Miller, *Textual Carnivals: The Politics of Composition*, 187

I

Without a doubt, the application of postmodern theory to the teaching of composition presents problems. In the prior chapter, we looked at some of the problems associated with border pedagogy, a postmodern approach for establishing relations of nonidentity with one's subject positions. These problems include confusing the critical process of nonidentification with the reactive step of disidentification. The subsequent effects of such confusion among students include approaching oneself as an artifact and engaging in excessive self-criticism. Although I have not argued for a retreat from the study of the hegemonic relations between discourse and subjectivity, I have argued that without a rich and sympathetic understanding of their investments in certain signs and signifiers, students (and their teachers) are likely to fall into writing formulas based on the ahistorical polarity of the false self and the true self. Having raised these problems and illustrated them, I have, it could be said, suggested caution against postmodern "theory hope." This suggestion of caution, however, is very different from the one offered by Stanley Fish in his essay, "Anti-foundationalism, Theory Hope and the Teaching of Composition."

In that essay, Fish attempts to disabuse anti-foundationalist critics of the hope that their commitment to a new epistemology will provide the basis for improved teaching. In particular, Fish directs his warning to teachers of composition, who, he says, have strong reasons to hope that the complementarity between anti-foundationalism and rhetoric will usher in an era of greater success in writing instruction. Defining anti-foundationalism as a theory that teaches the situationality of all "questions of fact, truth, correctness, validity and clarity" (344), Fish likens its claims to those that rhetoric has traditionally made for itself against philosophy— "claims of situation, history, politics and convention in opposition to the more commonly successful claims of logic, brute fact empiricism, the natural and the necessary" (347).

At the heart of Fish's argument against theory hope lies the following paradox: Because situationality is an *a priori* condition, all attempts to apply its lessons are subject to new situations that cannot be known or transcended. This prison-house of circumstance makes the attempt to study it absurd and hopeless. Writing, he argues, gets better—or doesn't—for banal reasons that are unrelated to the conscientious application of anti-foundationalist theories of meaning to the meaning-making concerns of composition. To the question, "Will the teaching of anti-foundationalism, to ourselves, and to our students, facilitate the teaching of writing," Fish answers "no" (348). In the end, this assertion of the nonrelation between theory and practice constitutes, for Fish, the ultimate working out of anti-foundationalist principles—the complete rejection of intellectual positivism and academic common sense. Indeed, for the academic who accepts the unusable nature of theory

Foundationalism Reworked

and who takes neither "comfort [nor] method from his creed," Fish reserves the title "anti-foundationalist hero" (354).

The unsentimental decisiveness of this position is attractive. Indeed, my discussion of Susan M.'s writing in the prior chapter could be said to support one of Fish's key points—that learning about our situatedness will not necessarily lead to our becoming "more self-consciously situated" or more "effective" in relation to it (347). However, if one takes a page from Fish's book and rejects "brute fact empiricism," then the application of anti-foundationalist theory to composition could be said to make as much sense as not applying it. But this Fishian conclusion—that it makes no difference one way or another—is one that I must also contest. Doing so requires that we look more closely at Fish's own argument.

Seemingly a *tour de force* of anti-foundationalist rug-pulling, Fish's essay ultimately relies on unexamined assumptions about the nature of good writing and good writing instruction which are oddly foundationalist in character in the way that they rest on an independent, stable conception of "the good." For instance, when alluding to E. D. Hirsh's recognition that we need to study the relations between literacy and culture in order to "do a good job," Fish (353) asks, "Does this mean that Hirsh wasn't doing a good job earlier?" By way of an answer, he writes, "I would venture to guess that he was as good a teacher of composition before he saw the contextual light as he is now" (353). Certainly, if it goes without saying what good writing is and hence what "doing a good job" always comes down to, then it makes sense that Fish would see Hirsh teaching to these essentials, one way or another. Excluding good writing from the effects of contextualism, however, he treats it as a foundational value.

In another instance of foundationalist thinking, Fish alludes to learning to write in terms that render it a self-evident and skills-based notion as in the following statement: "[I]nsofar as there has been and continues to be [a pedagogy based on maxims], many of the students submitted to it have learned to write" (354). Here, as elsewhere, the absence of student writing in the essay intensifies the foundationalist nature of the implied assertion that learning to write is a universally understood technical matter that needs no elaboration. Taking his point further about the capacity of maxims to teach writing, Fish does offer a subtle explanation regarding the power of tacit knowledge to render even the most debased methods (such as teaching by maxim) at least moderately effective. He continues: "[These students] have learned how to write in part because the maxims they are given are not explicit at all, in the sense of being detached from a tacitly known practice, but are the precipitations of a practice, whether they are presented as such or not" (354). Here Fish explains to us the way that the mental habits and discursive practices of a pervasive foundationalist ideology actually teach students "how to write," not the maxims or methods per se. But this insight is different from the one Fish intends, which is a more general statement about the inability of theory to teach us "how to write." Indeed, he would seem to be demonstrating the opposite—that dominant ideologies (such as foundationalism) are multiform and eminently effective. When what we are taught to think and write is relatively continuous with dominant social practices, the "how" will follow with only a tap, one way or another—maxims, modes of discourse, process—it hardly matters. It is in this sense alone that Fish's guess about Hirsh's teaching being equally effective, one way or another, makes sense.

Revising Fish's argument, we can thus state the following: The application of *anti*-foundationalist theories to the teaching of composition will not teach students "how to write" *foundationalist* discourse any better than traditional methods have. In other words, as long as phrases like "how to write" and "doing a good job" are taken for granted (and thus retain their foundationalist meaning), Fish will be correct in his discouragement of "theory hope." Only by refusing to talk about "how to write" before we talk about "what to write" do anti-foundational theorists working in composition have a chance to reinvigorate the discussion of where hope lies.[1] Indeed, the "brute fact" of anti-foundational theorists working in composition is that they have not, by and large, fallen into the error that Fish imagines of merely replacing "the components of the foundationalist world-picture with other components" (344). Specifically, anti-foundationalist teachers of writing have not assumed that teaching students "how to write" can be discussed as an independent, self-evident procedure, merely under revision. Rather, for such teachers of composition, "how to write" has been placed in dialectic with "what to write," the relationship being thus historicized in the name of a different, far less stable epistemology. Proponents of this new epistemology must set their own terms— develop their own rhetoric— or be condemned to negative judgment on the old terms of "effectiveness" in teaching students "how to write."

Not surprisingly, using the test of "effectiveness" on anti-foundationalist applications to foundationalist discourse, Fish finds them lacking. Gathering support for his conclusions from J. Hillis Miller, Fish cites from a 1983 essay that "empirical studies of the relative effectiveness of different theories of teaching are not . . . reassuring. They suggest that students will get somewhat better whatever the teacher does, perhaps through sheer praxis" (Fish, 1989: 354). What follows this statement in Miller's essay—qualification and counter-statement—Fish attributes to denial on Miller's part and a foundationalist nostalgia for principled relations between theory and practice. But counter-statement is not the same thing as reaction. Calling it reaction, however, releases Fish from having to account for Miller's continued interest in the application of anti-foundationalist theory to the teaching of composition, despite these studies. Since the reasons for Miller's continuing interest are relevant to the relationship between what to write and how to write, they warrant further consideration.

In his essay, "Composition and Decomposition" (1983), Miller argues that writing and reading are both rhetorics, the first being a "rhetoric of persuasion" and the second, "rhetoric as a knowledge of tropes" (43). As the two go hand in hand, they must be taught together. Miller devotes significant attention to the problems that result when the representative or tropological nature of language is ignored or simplified in writing texts. Citing a number of popular textbooks that treat metaphor as the ornamentation of literal language, Miller refers to the explanations made for such reductions— that the tropological nature of language is too complex for beginning students and would only "make things worse" (55). It is in this context that Miller draws faith in the "reasonableness of things" and invites Fish's rebuke. In particular, Miller continues to believe "that a thoroughly vitiated theory may come in one way or another to vitiate practice" (55). Making a claim for the slippery connection between how one writes and what one writes, here Miller is less the "foundationalist hero" than Fish who confers independent, timeless status on the notion of good writing (354). For his part, Miller refuses to be harassed by those empirical studies that report little difference in the effectiveness of various theories of writing. Instead, he shifts the terms of discussion away from their sole consideration on how to write to a concern for the relationship between the "what" and "how" of writing as in the following passage:

> To teach students the doctrine about figures I have found in these textbooks is like limiting classes in sex education to tales about the birds and the bees or like assuming in teaching young medical students that though the human body is in fact an organism it is simpler and more workable to tell students it is a wind-up mechanism.
> Teachers of writing and reading should take heart from the teachers of mathematics, biology and physics. Far from trying to hide from students the complexities of new developments in these disciplines, they have gone to work . . . from grade school on . . . to develop appropriate introductory courses. . . . [Teachers of writing and reading] should take the most advanced insights into language from both sides and attempt to work out commensurate pedagogies. (55)

By shifting our attention from effective to commensurate practices, Miller makes a contribution to the study of postmodern writing pedagogy, despite the fact that he continues to raise up ideals of "good" writing and reading as Randall Knoper has pointed out (1989: 130). In particular, Miller casts the debate over practice in terms of what we teach when we teach writing and why, rather than assuming there is nothing to discuss—the subject being self-evident, the methods tried and true. The difficulty of sustaining such a shift in attention cannot be overestimated. There are powerful historical motives for thinking about writing as a "neutral technology," motives that have been explored by literacy scholars in recent years (Trimbur 1991: 285). The more we understand about the power–knowledge relations shaping our assumptions regarding the timeless efficacy of "good writing," the less easy it becomes to accede to the atheoretical nature of composition as Fish would have it along with the "few worn bromides" that are left, such as:

Foundationalism Reworked 99

"practice makes perfect, you learn to write by writing, you must build on what you already know" (355).

Indeed, it could be argued that by equating "theory hope" with hope in anti-foundationalism, Fish has a rather easy case to make. Situationality, in Fish's essay, comes wrapped in the rhetoric of paradox, its versions developing circularly. For example, Fish argues that teaching situationality is paradoxically both impossible and inevitable: impossible because a "situation is always on the wing"; inevitable because "everything we teach is situational knowledge whether we label it so or not" (352). This is a morass, Fish warns, not to be taught directly. However, when this circular concept of situationality is replaced by a dialectical approach to the historicity of situation; when the paradoxes and tautologies of situationality are replaced by the analysis of history's contradictions and overdeterminations, the tautologies that Fish finds so absurd become—to borrow his preferred teaching alternative—fiercely ordinary. In short, contradiction and overdetermination are speculative instruments that give students a nonfoundational language for the effectivity of a structure in its effects (see Chapter 2) which Fish's emphasis on the static, universal nature of being-in-situation cannot. Paradoxically, access to such a language simplifies the work of students by giving them the material world to write about: in Freire and Macedo's terms, to read the world in the word. The study of "situationality," on the other hand, threatens merely to ratchet up expressionist modes of writing to new heights of self-consciousness, which Fish properly warns against.

Indeed, one could argue further that, despite the power of tacit knowledge to reinforce foundationalist approaches to reading and writing, students from all backgrounds have continued to disappoint generation after generation of writing instructors because (for one reason) foundationalism's resistance to history tortures its rhetoric and renders its overaestheticized forms of avoidance inaccessible to all but a relative few. On the other hand, when the comparatively simple notions of contradiction and overdetermination become the speculative instruments of student writers, far less "pedagogy," far less "application," is needed for students to go to work—less than would be the case with instruction in the static condition of situationality; less than is the case with instruction in "free self-expression." Of course, the fact that these speculative instruments are the acupuncture needles of Western literacy education means that they remain exotic and mistrusted for the most part. Focusing on this mistrust in her recent essay, "Marxist Ideas in Composition Studies" (1991), Patricia Bizzell writes that, while there may be less mistrust for Marxist ideas among American composition scholars than among some other academics, we nevertheless "do reflect the typical American willed blindness to Marxist thought... in our tendency to denature the Marxism of theorists whose work we use frequently" (53). This denaturing process often results in the teaching of perspectivism: students learn to take multiple perspectives on various issues and experiences without considering whose interests may be served by the various perspectives or by such a relativizing practice itself. By suppressing an analysis of the various power–knowledge relations at play, this process is truly denaturing: social inequality (contradiction) is separated from its multiple determinations, the latter staying on the table as the rather blander fare of multiple perspectives. The resistance that we find to a strong reading of contradiction and overdetermination, I would agree, is a sign of the times that Bizzell describes, not a result of their intrinsic nature.

Nevertheless, students do have a difficult time, as I have argued in earlier chapters, "making something of" the overdeterminations and contradictions they discern in regard to their situations. *This situation, understood as the inevitable tension they are experiencing between opposing epistemologies, is not in itself reason to quit the project.* Bizzell is particularly helpful on this account when she cites the following passage from Freire: "The role of critical pedagogy is not to extinguish tensions. The prime role of critical pedagogy is to lead students to recognize various tensions and enable them to deal effectively with them" (Freire and Macedo, 1987: 49). The tension that exists between epistemological approaches cannot be spared students without, as Freire indicates, depriving them of their own powers of agency. As I have also suggested, however, it is a mistake to assume that the study of overdetermination and contradiction *must* be conducted on particular sites. The distress that attends a vulgarly deterministic pedagogy is not the tension that Freire (or I) have in mind.

Rather, where the *double* activities of "learning about" and "making something of" social determinations are operating among students, critical education is taking place. Such education privileges the use-value of dialectical knowledge over its foundational-value, thus enacting a flexible, dialogic epistemology. The tension that we find between pedagogies directed toward the use-value of dialectical knowledge versus the foundational-value of dialectical knowledge can also be found throughout the history of literacy in general. When we study the forces that have tipped the scales in favor of the foundational values of knowledge against their use-values, we can also see familiar notions of "good writing" weighing in, notions that are always accompanied by an emphasis on "how-to write" at the expense of "what" to write and why.

Indeed, the histories of literacy and literacy crises supply ample motives for problematizing "good writing" and "good writing instruction" as foundational values and "neutral technologies." The presuppositions that continue to inform these notions virtually guarantee a continuing crisis, for they are at bottom exclusionary and thus failure-dependent. There is simply no getting around the fact that the educational apparatus's privileging of "good writing" has been at the expense of allowing students to develop a sense of authorship and a capacity to participate in public discourse. Further attention to this contradiction will help us to understand why we should shift our attention from *how* students write to *what* students write. In light of this understanding, Fish's plan for "building on what we already know" may not turn out to be the best advice.

In "Literacy and the Discourse of Crisis," John Trimbur traces the ways we have come to define schooled literacy by following the displacement of middle-class anxieties about its slipping status onto issues of language and schooling (1991: 280). Borrowing from Antonio Gramsci, Trimbur proceeds from the premise that whenever the "question of language" emerges as a social issue, other issues are about to emerge involving the reconsolidation of the dominant classes and the forms of amelioration they offer to the subordinate classes. Where language is in crisis, Gramsci argues, "the reorganization of cultural hegemony" is in process (quoted in Trimbur, 1991: 280). When Trimbur looks at a number of recent and not so recent American literacy crises, he finds that the middle class has been looking to education to guarantee its status and prerogatives at those times when larger economic and global forces threatened them. Even though they have been misplaced attempts to solve broader economic and social problems, these literacy crises have had consequences. One particularly important consequence has been the persistent narrowing of the notion of literacy to schooled literacy. A condensed and thoroughly institutionalized meaning has taken hold, giving public schooling great power as the moral and intellectual arbiter of individual success and failure (280). "Inspired by middle-class aspirations," Trimbur writes, "the discourse of literacy crises portrays the schooled literacy of public education simultaneously as an arena of equal opportunity for all who wish to enter and as an explanation of the success or failure of individuals in class society" (281). Looking to education to secure its future, the middle class has also used the educational apparatus to justify the social and economic inequality of individuals from subordinate groups.

Crucial to Trimbur's argument about the nonneutral uses of schooled literacy is the evidence he brings forward of another, popular version of literacy which gradually receded after wave upon wave of crisis. This version of literacy is not school-based. Trimbur writes: "Unlike the literacy of the common schools, popular literacy in the eighteenth and nineteenth centuries was largely a local phenomenon, embedded in everyday life, practical affairs, and political activities of family, workplace, and community" (288). Estimating an 80 percent literacy rate among free white men before mass public schooling, Trimbur ties the purposes of their literacy to nation-building and to the defense of democracy at local levels (288). Among slaves, a literacy rate ranging from 5 to 27 percent indicates that methods for resisting oppression included clandestinely learning to read and write (288). By contrast, the common-school movement, begun by Horace Mann, largely turned working literacy with its roots in participatory democracy and political resistance into rote literacy with its roots in discipline and character formation (289). Trimbur writes:

> The popular literacy of the early nineteenth century was a democratic tool, a literary and intellectual resource to know one's rights, to defend against monopolies and special interests, and to resist unjust and illegitimate authority. By mid-century, however, the extension of education through the

common schools appropriated the popular cultural force of literacy, domesticating and channeling it into controlled and regulated practices. (290)

By identifying schooled literacy with propriety and respectability, the developers of the common schools had a powerful tool to divide the classes in terms of their worth and moral stature. With the rise of progressive education in the early twentieth century, cognitive markers of literacy were developed, further dividing students, in the name of science this time rather than morality. Schooled literacy had now become a credentialing device, sharing in common with its morality-focused predecessor a largely measuring function. Taken together, the similarities between the moral and cognitive uses of literacy are greater than their differences, especially when compared with earlier forms of popular literacy "where the value of reading and writing had resided in their actual uses" (292).

It was precisely these "actual uses" that made the ruling classes ambivalent about literacy and that contributed to its control through schooling. When writing is taught largely as a matter of penmanship through the copying and memorizing of fixed passages, what is not being taught comes quickly to mind (289). So, too, when the teaching of grammatical correctness dominates language instruction, we can see that mass schooling is working not simply to broaden the middle class but to change what it might mean to be a member of it. Dividing the literate from the illiterate, mass schooling was simultaneously reducing the notion of literacy in ways that have significantly affected what we mean by "learning how to write."

Struggling to retain its faith in economic self-determinism even as monopoly capitalism changed the world of the petit bourgoisie, the middle class and those acceding to it have tended to put their faith in education and thus have suffered crises in faith, over and over again: literacy crises. As a result of these crises, education in general—reading and writing in particular—have come increasingly to be counted on as credentialing devices, the determiners of upward mobility (292). More and more the object of testing and measurement, literacy ranks individuals. No longer a set of context-specific, ever-transforming practices, literacy is now more often defined as discrete basic skills that reflect universal cognitive abilities. In an odd if not surprising twist, this increasing emphasis on literacy as the science of cognition has been used to measure worker character, more than even worker cognition. Citing the research of Kenneth Levine, Trimbur reports that literacy tests are used to screen workers whose service jobs are not likely to require even the reduced forms of literacy being tested. Instead, the tests serve "as a 'proxy' to assess cooperativeness, reliability, and trainability" (285).

In short, the history of how to read and how to write is a history inseparable from the desires and insecurities of the middle class and its displacements of these thwarted desires and mounting insecurities onto the teaching of literacy. As a tool for guaranteeing upward mobility, literacy has become the imaginary marker of an individual's social viability even as its decontextualized schooled version has made it increasingly unrelated to social life. Rather than "enlarging the public sphere of discourse and political participation," schooled literacy is a form of "cultural capital," part of what Trimbur calls "a wider ideology of possessive individualism" (294).

In this light, Fish's disinterest in the question of *what* we teach when we teach "good writing" seems an avoidance of a painfully important subject. Indeed, the work of Susan Miller, James Berlin, Gerald Graff, Douglas Wallace, and others confirms that the trends in public schooling highlighted by Trimbur can be extended to higher education. Lest we think that the reductive approaches to literacy which characterize public schooling do not apply to postsecondary education, we have only to look at the history of composition in the "new" university for proof that they, in fact, do apply. Tracing the birth of English studies at Harvard under its president, Charles William Eliot, Susan Miller finds that its mission, defined in terms of both literature and composition, used composition to check and correct the worthiness of those young men whose social class backgrounds represented a broader spectrum than the old university had. In 1873, Miller writes, English composition at Harvard would "instill in the nonelect the necessary refinements of taste, in the form of correct grammar and spelling, two historically important forms of cultural propriety that Harvard's way of teaching was going to provide" (1991: 52). The puritanical linkage between election and correctness which Trimbur finds coloring the meaning of literacy in the common schools takes a similar tint in the composition practices of the new universities. Refuting those histories that assert composition's distorted yet continuous relationship with classical rhetoric, Miller argues instead that freshman composition was founded "as a consciously selected menu to test students' knowledge of graphic conventions, to certify their propriety, and to socialize them into academic good manners" (66). As the "low" work of English departments, it derived its importance from its absolute difference from the "high" work of literary study: writing for correctness among freshmen was completely different from writing for authorship among literary geniuses—but also completely necessary. It is not hard to see how freshman writing, institutionalized as "not-literature" and received as always already wrong, works against its future applications or transformations in spheres of practical writing. In other words, the teaching of writing on the Harvard model militated against the actual practice of writing. Discounting the idea that students could or should write whole pieces of timely, responsive prose, the new composition course was, according to Miller, "a national course in silence" (55).

It is a given of contemporary composition studies that process pedagogy can give students back their voices by putting them in touch with their own perspectives and generative capacities. However, Miller raises doubts about this assumption by demonstrating the continuity of process pedagogy with earlier approaches to freshman writing instruction. These previous approaches decontextualized the making of meaning and rendered it an intransitive process. Earlier still, in the "old" university, students had used textbooks that taught particular, popular genres of discourse such as business, news and personal letters, fiction, essays, histories of law, scientific prose, and criticism. However, with the rise of the "new" university, these public categories disappeared (60). In their place came the modes of discourse and the study of forms apart from precipitating situations. For all their differences, the modes can be compared with contemporary process pedagogy in the way that both have had students writing for inward purposes about personal rather than public matters, recalling a character-building, moralistic function for writing rather than a socially engaged, rhetorical function. Like the modes, so, too, process pedagogy inculcates an "intransitive," "self-referential" (97) subject of writing which Miller argues has helped to continue familiar forms of alienation from the public uses of writing: "The composition student is expected to experience processes, activities, strategies, multiple perspectives, peer groups, and evaluations that have no articulated relation to actual results from a piece of writing" (100).

When "good writing" is equated with these decontextualized processes, a contradiction ensues which deserves our attention: the exclusive student-centeredness of such methods actually disentitles its practitioners from recognizing and understanding the relational functions of writing. This institutionalization of a genre of "unentitled" writing is at the heart of Miller's critique of freshman composition and its rise to disciplinary status. Although her analysis does indeed support Fish's skepticism of process pedagogy as the new "hope" of composition, it does not confirm his larger argument that good writing is a timeless practice that theory cannot affect. On the contrary, Fish's anti-foundationalist argument, as it comes full circle to invoke such nineteenth-century notions as "practice makes perfect," confirms Miller's and Trimbur's thesis that contemporary freshman writing instruction continues a damaging historic pattern whereby the ever more correct and refined practice of written expression represents an individual quest for upward mobility and personal election. Certainly, Miller has a point when she argues that this solipsistic and ultimately pacifying function that has so notoriously come to be condensed in the institution of composition can, and most appropriately should, be resisted by composition studies (187).

Educated to revere the importance of surface correctness and to accept huge amounts of decontextualized work toward their credentialing, both current and future generations of composition students need to be invited, slowly, into a new counterhegemonic writing project. The purposes, broadly speaking, of such a project are dual: to analyze the social functions of their current reading and writing practices and the subject positions they define; and to reconstruct these practices for different social functions and subject positions, as they can and as they choose. By using writing to discern the lineaments of their "situations," composition students would not be subjected to lessons in "how to write." Instead, they would be working the writing that has been working them—studying, in various contexts, what this writing does, how it does it, and what the available or yet-to-be imagined alternatives might be.

II

Each chapter in this book has discussed and illustrated different aspects of such a counterhegemonic writing project. The fact that contradictions still exist among the chapters is a regrettable but unavoidable symptom of my own uneven relationship to this huge and difficult undertaking, one that many others in the field are also working on. There can be no final mastery of this counterhegemonic practice, no unified pedagogy to submit once and for all. In the prior chapters, I have defined and described those rudiments of a dialogic and dialectic practice that I think may be useful to others as they shape their own projects.

In the first section of this chapter, I reviewed Stanley Fish's influential argument against theory's usefulness to teaching students how to write and pointed out a contradiction: Fish's antifoundational argument against "theory hope" rests, ultimately, on foundational notions of good writing and good writing instruction. What makes this contradiction of more than passing interest as a logical problem can be found in the history of literacy instruction in the United States, as that history has been influenced by similar assumptions about good writing as a timeless value and a neutral skill. Even a brief look at this history of literacy reveals the extent to which these assumptions have led to methods that emphasize writing for personal correctness at the expense of writing for popular use, and to the equation of such correctness with moral virtue and social viability. Because these disciplinary standards and pacifying methods have tended to disentitle students from using writing in public and transactional ways, there is reason to question whether Fish's reliance on these traditional notions of good writing as timeless values and neutral skills is, as he believes, in the best interest of students.

Having concluded the first section with a broad endorsement of an alternative practice that counters these traditional approaches and the foundational theories on which they rest, I may appear, by comparison, to have rather modest purposes for this second section. These purposes can be stated in the form of the following questions: What may be in store for instructors who are not willing to fall back on Fish's "few worn and familiar bromides" to teach composition, but who have not yet developed a rich, interlocking network of counterhegemonic practices to structure their work? How can such instructors proceed?

In this section, I attempt a counterhegemonic response to these questions, using student writing not so much to illustrate the mixed effects of one's practice at this stage as much as to theorize it. Doing so, I would hope to suggest, along with Susan Miller, Lester Faigley, and others, that for an instructor engaged in such a counterhegemonic practice there is more to do with student writing than to judge its relationship to our intentions. Rather, students who are engaged in the problematization of their discourse practices can be seen to be working as researchers, producing texts that explore the complex network of social relations constituting their literacy *in its effects*. Confronted with research that details the densely situated nature of their literacy-in-progress (as students understand it and are willing to represent it), the writing instructor who wants to go beyond the foundational premises embedded in the notion "how to write" is given powerful support.

From the brief sketch I have given of schooled literacy in the United States, three foundational premises stand out which pressure writing instructors at every level of alternative practice. These premises can be stated as follows: (1) The composition student is a child-subject, always a beginner to literacy practices; (2) the site and pacing of these practices are controlled by the educator working from a developmental model of linear progress; and (3) the correctly paced interventions of instructors can bring students to a common point of arrival based on their common point of departure as child-subjects. That all of these premises have been fiercely contested by proponents of process, and that they have, to a considerable degree, been reincorporated as process, attests to their residual vigor. On the other hand, when composition students write themselves out of those premises by articulating their presence as historical subjects already in a network of discursive practices, an instructor also has a chance to continue writing herself out of that script as well and into a new form of dialogue with the students.

Although this rhetorical use of student research may be less than Trimbur and Miller imagine for the emergence of transitive writing and entitled writers, I would argue that, for some instructors at least, as well as graduate students-in-training, it may be an historically necessary aspect of its development. Under present circumstances, any counterhegemonic writing project is likely to be a tension-filled learning process. Instructors will have to struggle continually with their own investments in the premises of traditional writing pedagogy toward the building of alternative commitments and alternative subject positions. As with our students, the pressure toward premature disidentification with old subject positions and the subsequently superficial, even fatuous, adoption of new ones is a threat. For this reason, I am emphasizing the slowness and unevenness of this process, for instructors and students alike.

Texts that attest to a student's already political, already historical subjectivity demand a commensurate response. Such a response cannot reasonably be less in touch with the overdetermined relations shaping students' reading and writing practices than the students themselves are. Student writing thus takes a more genuinely transitive form than is customary: it instructs the instructors on the subject of hegemonic discourse relations and persuades them to pursue a practice commensurate with the lessons of these papers. Instructors who learn to use student writing in this way are also beginning to recognize a different subjectivity for the writing student than the customary subjectivity that Richard Ohmann memorably describes as "classless," "sexless," and "timeless" (1976: 145).

By way of illustration, consider the rhetorical effects of the following student writing on the instructor who is struggling with the enduring influence of the premises listed above and with a lingering belief in the timeless capacity of good writing to improve one's social viability. This excerpt, from a paper called "Feelings of Entitlement," addresses the assignment described in Chapter 3 where the students are asked to read Robert Coles's essay and to name their own entitlements in relation to his discussion. The first four paragraphs of Dozi O.'s seven-paragraph paper read as follows:

I am a U.S. citizen by place of birth, but a Nigerian by nationality. I spent the first four years of my life in the U.S. before I went home to Nigeria. This was in the 70's, 1977 to be precise; when living or being born abroad was a big deal, a great privilege worth to be envied by others.

I used to be a quiet, timid, nice boy, owing to the way my parents brought me up. But as I started to realise and acknowledge the attention, the respect so to speak, I got from other kids of my age in school, at church and also at the playground even from older people and my teachers. I developed and began to nourish a thought, a kind of new awareness that there was something great about me. This changed me dramatically. I started to look down on the close friends I had. I became pompous and kind of disrespectful. This change of attitude, though gradual, was noticed by my school teachers and parents as well. It kind of became a big problem in that the character I portrayed was alien to what is known of my family. My mother feared that this attitude,where ever it came from would destroy my character.

As time went by, I lost most of my friends. The prestige and attention I thought I had was gone, the wheel was turned around and I was looked upon as a snob. Formerly, I used to wait for my friends to greet me first whenever we met. I made it a habit to ignore them if they did not first say hi. This caused them to start ignoring me too. Teachers that once had me as their favorates began to dislike me because of the proud and impolite manner in which I spoke. On one accasion, I had the guts to call a teacher by his name instead of saying "sir" and to my greatest surprise, he wipped me with his cane. It was not the fact that he used the cane on me that surprised me, I just could not Imagine that happening to me.

Well, looking at those circumstances now that I'm of age (18 years to be precise) that attitude that later wore off with time and due to events, was not my fault. Putting into consideration a kid my age at that time (between 5 and 9 years old) having to deal with all the adoration and attention I had. In fact being treated as a king and gazed on like a piece of silver. I just couldn't help it.

Foundationalism Reworked

Present for a teacher here is an array of circumstances shaping Dozi's relations to his current studies in an American university. A Nigerian-American for whom the hyphenation misrepresents the fractured relations between these subjectivities, Dozi challenges all three of composition's traditional premises by virtue of his representation of his situation. The layers of political experience which he records describe a subject in a network of social relations that defy the models of linear development posited by composition and the corresponding forms of teacher control over his uses of literacy. Read rhetorically, Dozi instructs the instructor in regard to the mixed effects that any pedagogical intervention is likely to have on him. Along with an enduring sense of his entitlement as an American, which he describes in a later section, he also retains the memory of the ostracism this has caused him at the hands of his parents, teachers, and friends. Having read about Phillis Wheatley's "contrary instincts" earlier in the term, Dozi presents to his current teacher his own contrary instincts regarding the entitlements of American citizenship. Just as Alice Walker reviews the names applied to Wheatley for having written adoringly of her mistress as the fair-haired "Goddess" (Bartholomae and Petrosky, 1987: 611) so too Dozi, in a later section, reviews the names applied to him in high school for his Western ways: "Friends who knew my line of thinking called me names like 'London Goat' and 'Yankee Fool' and so on."

Continuing to analyze the circumstances that have "entitled" him to an isolation that includes both feelings of superiority and aloneness, Dozi makes it hard to imagine that any action on behalf of his development as an acceptably literate American college student will not also, to some degree, contribute to his education as a "Yankee Fool." This at least can be seen as one of the challenges presented by Dozi's discussion of his literacy in context. Of course, there are also signs in the essay that the methods for contextualization and the language for contradiction which he is learning are welcome instruments of agency and mediation. Just as Walker says to Wheatley, "But at last, Phillis, we understand" (611), so, too, Dozi writes to himself, his teacher, and his peers that, all things considered, it "was not my fault . . . I just couldn't help it." The striking reference he makes to being "of age" also suggests that he sees himself now as authorized to begin shaping his own history, rather than only being painfully divided by it.

Such writing, I am arguing, because it situates students as subjects of complex, discursive histories, can materially alter an instructor's lingering commitments to the very different premises of literacy's traditional values and the subject positions they imply. When it does, so, too, have the positions of the students been affected. Whether these effects constitute the beginning of new commitments among the students can never be clear. What is clear, however, is that unless the writing includes this subtle rhetorical effect on the instructor, it will never become transitive for the student, within *that* classroom, in other ways either. Thus, I feel compelled to pause at this ambiguous intersection of residual and emergent practices and to study it further—precisely because it is as little written about as I imagine it is frequently experienced.

In *Marxism and Literature* (1977), Raymond Williams writes, "Hegemony is always an active process" (115). By extension we can add: Counterhegemony is always an active process too. As such, it is always going to be a complex, even dismaying mix of residual and emergent elements whose relationships to one another are unstable and shifting. "It is exceptionally difficult," writes Williams, "to distinguish between . . . elements of some new phase of the dominant culture . . . and those which are substantially alternative or oppositional to it: emergent in the strict sense, rather than merely novel" (123). One reason why it is so difficult to make this distinction, explains Williams, is that the residual elements of dominant practices are not archaic relics of the past. They have been reformed for present use and thus are "actively residual" (123). In addition, their present function may also include oppositional aspects along with predominantly traditional ones. It is not hard to see how process pedagogy fits this mixed description. Although it may be true that process pedagogy incorporates traditional forms of student subjectivity, it is also evident that by bringing dialectics into writing, a process approach does invite alternative forms of subjectivity to emerge in some settings. If it is impossible to determine or predict what the exact social function of a particular practice will be, it is also impossible to be purely counterhegemonically aligned.

Foundationalism Reworked

Thus, the very concept of a "counterhegemonic practice" is an idealism. Such a practice will always consist of residual and emergent elements, and these elements themselves will not maintain a fixed status. For these reasons, it could be argued that the ambiguous circumstances of the instructor who is beginning a counterhegemonic practice stands for the circumstances of every other counterhegemonic instructor, writ large. The undecidability and deep historicity of every aspect of such a project is something that instructors need to immerse themselves in. Otherwise, as I have indicated, there can be no change in an instructor's own subject position which is open enough to history's power and supple enough in its face to carry out a project in a way that really has anything to do with students' enhanced subjectivities and critical capacities. Possibly because the process of significantly shifting one's own subject position is so very slow and so very ambiguous, anti-foundationalist critics such as Stanley Fish, Richard Ohmann, and Victor Vitanza have questioned the wisdom of applying the results of one's own repositioning to the classroom. Observing the way exhortations and problem-solving formats still creep into the counterhegemonic research of his fellow composition scholars, Ohmann writes bemusedly that "hegemony mocks some of our best efforts" (1991: XV).

Less bemused in his criticism of such inconsistencies between theory and application is Victor Vitanza. His essay, "Three CounterTheses: Or, A Critical In(ter)vention into Composition Theory and Pedagogy," is intended to be an enactment of postmodern discourse, an effort at nonidentification with traditional subject positions. By example and by declaration, he calls for a moratorium on applications, arguing (among other things) that without significantly deeper alterations in our own subject positions and the discourses they interpellate, such applications cannot be anything more than paratheoretical: "The field of composition demonstrates a resistance *to* theory by rushing to apply theory to praxis without ever realizing the resistance *of* theory itself to be theorized and applied. . . . Theory has become, for the field of composition, the will to unified theory" (160).

Taking these criticisms seriously, I am nevertheless inclined in a different direction. Eschewing Vitanza's Lyotardian imperative to "just drift" (151) while recognizing the wisdom of his and Ohmann's warning against a mawkish application of theory which positions the instructor now as the master of *oppositional* subjectivity, I would respond in the following way: Working with students and their writing to continue effecting one's own subjectivity as an instructor is not the same as "applying"—or misapplying—theory from a position of mastery. Rather, it represents a recognition that "application" and the master/disciple positions that correspond to it are effects of cultural hegemony. Instead of reproducing those effects whole cloth, students and instructors can become readers of them—working the theories that are working them, in the manner of Foucault's specific intellectuals, who, by virtue of the difficulty and concreteness of this work for both are neither masters nor disciples.

As I stated earlier, the instructor who wants to go beyond the traditional premises contained in the notion "how to write" must slowly and seriously rebuild her own subjectivity as a classroom instructor. Learning to receive student writing transitively is a means toward this end. Calling for a "moratorium" or a month of Sundays to get it right before going into the classroom, however, completely misses the point of theory's presence in its effects. James Berlin is particularly helpful on this matter, arguing that teaching does not follow theory as its pale imitator. "Instead," he writes, "the classroom becomes the point at which theory and practice engage in a dialectical interaction, working out a rhetoric more adequate to the historical moment and the actual conditions of students and teachers" (*Poststructuralism*, 25).

Toward the realization of this dialectic, I would argue that the practice of receiving student writing transitively plays a large part, one that Fish does not consider here in relation to composition, despite his affiliation with reader–response theory. Receiving student writing transitively can alter a teacher's subjectivity in ways that reading *about* the effects of hegemonic discourse relations from published authors alone cannot. Historically, a teacher's relationship to a student paper is evaluative and authoritative. The pen moves in response to a student's strengths and weaknesses in terms of *our* uses for his literacy. Reading Richard Rodriguez, Maxine Hong Kingston, Mike Rose, or Michel Foucault, for that matter, cannot alone still the pen's conventional work on an essay like Dozi's. The teacher must also come to understand (and this may take years) that Dozi's essay itself disrupts the pen's conventional work by hailing a different kind of reader. In making this comment, I do not mean to imply a dichotomy between academic and personal responses to a student's text. I do mean to say that when a paper hails a teacher as what Shoshana Felman calls a student of the student's knowledge, the teacher is working as an active historical subject, participating in an actual literate event (1982: 33). Only as a teacher works in this way, day after day, student after student, can her own discursive practices change in relation to her students', thereby "forging a rhetoric more adequate to the historical moment" (Berlin, *Poststructuralism*, 25).

In the process of working out a rhetoric "more adequate to the historical moment," a teacher confronts over and over again how nonlinear and nondevelopmental her interventions must be. Antifoundationalism creeps in the back door in the guise of experience, causing changes in one's subject position to feel like common sense. While sharing certain discursive and social features that can be called common points of departure, students also begin to diverge so greatly in so many ways for such an instructor that a common point of arrival seems possible only when it is reduced to issues of surface correctness and basic skills. Over time, it becomes apparent that composition's traditional function of standardizing students actually works against the students' acquisition of the standard, academic uses of literacy by mistaking standards of form with standards of development. By helping students to acquire and to interanimate critically the different languages of heteroglossia, the anti-foundationalist instructor may paradoxically be more successful in teaching academic discourse than the foundationalist instructor who concentrates on academic discourse alone in an uncritical, decontextualized way. This payoff, so to speak, of embedded, dialogical learning may come over time as one learns to read student writing transitively.

In the following paper by an advanced composition student who prefers anonymity, it is possible to see many of the effects I have been discussing come together. One can see the student instructing the instructor regarding his historical subjectivity. By virtue of the particular uses he is able to make of the course in *his* context, the writer reminds the instructor of the unpredictable network of discursive practices she is entering and how very dependent her interventions are on this context. Titling his work "The Diverse Meanings of Diversity," the author reflects the assignment that was to develop a radial reading of some issue or experience in relation to John Berger's concept of "radial knowledge." Radial knowledge, we will recall from Chapter 2, is Berger's term for overdetermined methods of cultural analysis. By looking at aspects of culture personally, politically, economically, dramatically, and historically, and by recognizing the nonidentity of these perspectives, Berger suggests that one may begin to supplant unilinear approaches to meaning and unilinear notions of self. In the first three paragraphs below, the author looks radially at his experiences in Alcoholics Anonymous. What he finds is an economically and culturally diverse group of people who are expected to suppress their historical differences in the interest of a common purpose: recovery. His conflict over what is gained and what is lost by such a unilinear approach establishes a context for his later discussion of campus diversity. He writes:

> I was once a part of a diverse group of people. Men and women, blacks and whites, Hispanics, people from the upper classes, working classes, even skid row bums, homosexuals and lesbians too: these people were my friends and the fellowship was Alcoholics Anonymous. We all shared a common problem, alcoholism, and a common goal, to stay sober. I remember how peculiar it was listening to a white, middle class businessman talk about how he would be drunk from a party the night before while he was planning a corporate merger or new promotional campaign, and five minutes later listen to an African American welfare recipient take the podium and talk about how the craving for alcohol, in a very real sense, forced her to spend her monthly relief check on booze instead of food for her children. While the stories were often alien, we tried to extract something from the stories that we could relate to, that we could take home and think about so that we could gain a better understanding of our alcoholism. Whether it was guilt from having hurt most the ones we loved, doing shameful things that we would never imagine ourselves doing, or trying to keep track of the vicious circle of lies that we surrounded ourselves with for protection, we

all could find something that we shared in common with the speaker.

The only formal requirement was a desire to stop drinking, but there were also many unspoken rules—rules that were necessary to avoid conflict. I remember one meeting when a man started discussing his childhood that was nothing but one horrible episode of sexual abuse after another. All of a sudden, the smoke-filled, caffinated roomful of people clammored for the man to stay with the alcohol-related issues. I'm not sure if I was uncomfortable because of the man's story or because of the censorship. Alcoholics Anonymous does have some elements of indoctrination. Yet I believe, as I was taught, that alcohol is but a symptom . . . an alcoholic doesn't drink for the pleasure, at least not in the end, but drinks to escape. What is apparent to me now is a contradiction. Most of the speakers discussed in extremely vague language the circumstance of their lives, but talked at length on universal emotions. By omission, their stories became remarkably similar.

If the African American mentioned earlier was to take the podium and discuss the politics of welfare, how the system perpetuates itself by not offering any real opportunity to its recipients, and how this system aided her feelings of hopelessness (a feeling almost all alcoholics feel) that fueled her alcoholism, I doubt the group would be very tolerant. My intention is not to denegrade AA. On the contrary, I owe my life to the organization. But then I'm not sure how much of this belief is a result of indoctrination or whether the belief is the result of sincere gratitude. My point here, however, is simply that one of the ways AA survives is that as a whole, the group is very careful about discussing issues, even avoiding issues that may cause conflict. Maintaining diversity, at least in my experience attending meetings for more than five years, has a price.

On the basis of his reading of his experiences in AA, the author goes on to make distinctions among a number of academic discourses he has encountered about diversity. In so doing, he arrives at a point where he is able to develop a powerful perspective on the contradictions and possibilities of his current education. It is worth noting that the writer's facility with the discourses he alludes to is inseparable from his critical, dialogical relationship to them. By virtue of this critical, dialogical relationship, his writing would seem to resemble the popular literacy that Trimbur describes as an adaptive, "democratic tool" for everyday life more than it resembles the typically disengaged, declamatory forms of schooled literary.

In the two paragraphs that follow those above, the author shifts venues and reflects on his matriculation at the University of Massachusetts–Boston, eight years after entering AA. Noticing the diversity of students and its resemblance to the cross section he saw in AA, the author says that in itself this range of students is only a start. The University, he writes, goes beyond the "superficial diversity" touted in catalogues and advertisements by encouraging students to look at issues in the terms Berger suggests as "simultaneously personal, political, economic, dramatic, everyday and historical" (1980: 63). One illustration the author provides of such a radial approach comes from his psychology class. Skillfully adapting its discourses to his purposes, he writes:

> Virtually every theory the professor presents in her lecture is deconstructed to reveal the context surrounding the birth of the theory. Theory, I suspect she would say, is not created in a vacuum, and perhaps the same is true of education. When the class was learning about intelligence and testing, the professor lectured on the usual stuff, who invented the first intelligence test, how accurate the test was, the formulas used to determine the scores and other basic information. Then she passed out an excerpt from Leon Kamin's book entitled *The Science and Politics of I.Q.* This very different perspective on intelligence testing totally contradicted the information she provided in the lecture. Now, the testing seemed brutal, void of any scientific value. Kamin quoted Lewis Termin, the major translator of the intelligence test developed by Alfred Binet in France, defining the purpose of the testing. The quote is so shocking I'll include it in full:
>
> > ... in the near future intelligence testing will bring tens of thousands of these high-grade defectives under the surveillance and protection of society. This will ultimately result in curtailing the

Foundationalism Reworked

reproduction of feeble-mindedness and in the elimination of an enormous amount of crime, pauperism and industrial inefficiency. (Kamin 6)

Kamin goes on to explore Termin's connection with eugenics groups, and keeps up a relentless pace linking such issues as underclass sterilization and immigration control to the new Americanized Stanford-Binet intelligence test. The point I'm trying to make is not about intelligence testing as a means of social control, but rather that U.Mass-Boston's approach to teaching contributes more toward the goal of diversity than quotas or non-traditional course offerings.

At this point of his essay, having fulfilled the assignment to assess an aspect of his experience in radial terms, the author goes on to enlarge it. He enters into the debate developing on campus at the time regarding the institution of a diversity requirement. Having critically interanimated five meanings of diversity—that of AA, Berger, the university administration, his composition course (not included here), and his psychology course—the author begins to imagine a public function for his writing. In peer review, he reported that his essay was turning into a position paper against the diversity requirement under discussion in the college. In his paper, he argues as follows:

> The fact that the university doesn't have this non-traditional requirement is not really a contradiction to its claim of diversity. As suggested earlier diversity is more than requirements and quotas. Indeed, there are diverse meanings of diversity. As I've experienced in AA, it is possible to have all outward appearance of diversity, yet be intolerant in the process, intolerant in the name of diversity. Quotas and course requirements are not as risky as school administrators claim. Enforced diversity comes from an anonymous authority, the administration, and the non-traditional courses they require could very well be taught in traditional, non-diverse ways. If the course material is not held up to the same critical analysis as traditional courses are, and if the material is taught in a non-dialogical way, the possibility of conflict is lessened in much the same way AA does through its many unspoken

rules. So, I am cautious when any group, school, or association uses the diversity buzzwords "access," "non-Western," and "minority requirement." Instead, I look to how these vehicles for diversity are implemented. This, I think, is the real test for diversity.

Of course, certain responses can be made to this argument, and they were made. There is, in fact, now a diversity requirement on the University of Massachusetts–Boston campus. In the context of this chapter, however, I am interested in what this paper can teach us about reclaiming the public uses of literacy for college writing which we see this student inching toward. Through the critical interanimation of the various diversity discourses that he has encountered, the writer begins to define a space for rhetorical action that fits his present constellation of competencies and interests. Although course readings and assignment sequences must also be devised to encourage such popular uses of literacy, the fact that such materials will still be used in a classroom context means that the traditional relationship between writing teacher and writing student will militate residually against the transformation of school writing for popular, rhetorical use. That is why I have tried to emphasize in this chapter that the popular, rhetorical uses of literacy in composition cannot just be a project for students. It must also be a project for teachers, one that begins with their reception of student writing as a social text from which they may learn about the network of literacy relations into which they are entering—its themes, limits, and possibilities. Indeed, the history of composition shows us that some of the most pungent criticism directed against the field has occurred when teachers have "taught" rhetoric without themselves having any actual, rhetorical relationship to what their students write. It would seem that when the normalizing, intransitive function of traditional composition instruction is linked with rhetoric, a particularly strange, hybrid form results, one that, to say the least, bears some review.

For Roger Sale, writing in 1970, one result of this linkage was "the fallacy of the arguable proposition," defined as the fallacy "that a proposition, simply because it is arguable is therefore worth arguing" (49). These decontextualized exercises in argumentation—which instructors could evaluate according to standards of evidence and then drop—are what Richard Ohmann, in 1976, found textbook authors teaching and which he renamed "pseudo-argument": "[O]ut of history, the imagined writer and reader of these texts are prophylactically sealed in an environment of disinterestedness" (1976: 158, 156). But even when readings and assignment sequences are developed to engage students' interests in defining social uses for their literacies, the composition classroom will not diverge from its tendency toward standardized, intransitive forms of writing, including the pseudo-argument, unless the subjectivities of teachers and students become actively historical and thus actually rhetorical. From Felman's psychoanalytic point of view, this means that, unless the position of the teacher is "the position of the one who learns," the students will never exercise their capacities to teach (37).

In "The Diverse Meanings of Diversity," the writer demonstrates how to read transitively across the borders of his discourses; in so doing, he has begun to effect a new subject position for himself *and* his instructor. By virtue of both working in less bounded, monologic, personal ways, their work has become social and transactional. For the student, rhetoric has not returned as a new "bounded" form—as pseudo-argument—but as the literate action of a faceted self. For the instructor, rhetoric has not returned as arguable propositions to be graded but as a receptivity to student discourse as "knit into the whole belief structure of its holder" (Ohmann, 1976: 156). Such emergence by composition students and teachers into more immediate, rhetorical relations goes against the grain of schooled literacy traditions. As these traditions are reproduced most powerfully in teacher–student relations, only as they are transformed will the writing also be transformed. The difficulties that are present for *both* in trying to understand the hegemonic traditions they are in the midst of do not, as Ohmann feared years later, necessarily result in contradictions that mock our best efforts. Rather, the circumstance I am positing in dialogue with the student above—where both teachers and students begin to concede their historicity and learn, though in different ways, what kinds of subject positions follow—may, for once, mock hegemony. Under these circumstances, composition students may begin to imagine actual, popular uses for their literacies. Thus, they may effect a new critical rhetoric in dialogue with a teacher who is herself learning to read students' literacies as always already popular—as always already pamphlets put in one's hand to disrupt one's day teaching students "how to write."

NOTE

1. After drafting this chapter, I discovered that this distinction between how to write and what to write can be found in a number of other works of composition theory: see, for example, Faigley, 1992; Knoper, 1989; and White, 1984.

Epilogue: Working the "Specific Reality of Discourse"

> The principle of *specificity* declares that a particular discourse cannot be resolved by a prior system of significations; that we should not imagine that the world presents us with a legible face, leaving us merely to decipher it; it does not work hand in glove with what we already know.... We must conceive discourse as a violence that we do to things, or at all events, as a practice we impose upon them; it is in this practice that the events of discourse find the principle of their regularity.
>
> —Michel Foucault, "The Discourse on Language,"
> *The Archaeology of Knowledge*, 228

Just as Foucault substitutes the concept of the specific intellectual for the traditional concept of the universal intellectual, so, too, he substitutes the principle of discourse specificity for the older concept of discourse universality. Precisely because "a particular discourse cannot be resolved by a prior system of significations," specific intellectuals must analyze the theories of knowledge and systems of truth that are working the multiple discourses of their fields toward their resolution based on distance and difference, not identity. Having redefined knowledge and truth as worldly systems materialized in language, specific intellectuals do not simply "use" language as a neutral or transparent medium of expression. Rather, they *work* language for an understanding of its particular effects on knowledge and truth. In "The Discourse on Language,"

Foucault calls this an understanding of "the specific reality of discourse" and argues that such understanding has been largely excluded from Western philosophy since the fall of the Sophists. In its place, he writes, "Western thought has seen to it that discourse be permitted as little room as possible between thought and words" (1972a: 227).

By reclaiming the principle of discourse specificity, students and teachers of composition are also in the position to reclaim the historical and appropriative role of the specific subject. For such a subject, the spaces between "thought and words," between systems of signification, between events and their meanings, are zones of contention among unequal forces with which a critical subject must begin to engage. What we have seen Bakhtin call "relativized consciousness" toward "internally persuasive" discourse relations, Foucault would call the specific intellectual's work with the ensembles of discursive events structuring a field. It is at the junctures of these discursive events that relativized consciousness of language difference is called for precisely because "a particular discourse *cannot* be resolved by a prior system of significations" (emphasis mine). However, at those junctures, where one has the most composing to do, traditional approaches to language leave one least equipped to do it. It has been the argument of this book—introduced in Chapter 1—that composition scholars need to develop themselves and their students as experts on the conjunctural effects of the various competing discourses, constructing their relations to work and school, self and society. Finding specific methods for understanding and acting on these conjunctural effects remains the challenge for literacy education today.

In this epilogue, I will review the dominant themes that obstruct both an understanding of discourse specificity and the development of a commensurate practice in order that I may also present principles for opening up discourse to a perception of its specificity. In relation to these themes and counter-principles, I will discuss the text of a freshman writer whose stories as a missionary and an English/Haitian-Creole translator can help to bring these themes and counter-principles into focus. By so doing, I hope to bring new context and immediacy to the argument of this book as a whole—that in composition studies today both students and teachers need to work the theories that are working them toward their own critical becoming as readers and interpreters of discourse's specific effects.

Three themes have historically supported the denial of the specific reality of discourse in Western thought. Foucault lists these themes as follows: (1) the founding subject; (2) the originating experience; and (3) the universal mediation (1972a: 227–28). For the founding subject, language is a tool for building meaning, a flexible set of bricks and blocks for realizing one's self-originating goals. "The task of the founding subject," writes Foucault, "is to animate the empty forms of language with his objectives" (227). These self-originating objectives, foisted upon language, have their corollary in the foundational meaning contained in the object of inquiry. For every founding subject, there is an originating experience made to fit. "Things murmur meanings" to the founding subject, writes Foucault, which language "has merely to extract" (228). In other words, for the founding subject in relation to the originating experience, language acts as a go-between, a universal mediator with no historical or material force of its own. Together these themes reduce discourse to the mere status of "signs." "It is as though," Foucault writes, "people have wanted to efface all trace of [discourse's] irruption into the activity of our thought and language" (228). Given the long history of this effacement through the construction of sturdy, traditional beliefs about language, self, and meaning, it would be hard to overestimate the counter-memory needed to challenge them. Indeed, since these deep-rooted, foundational themes can only be countered by nonfoundational principles of discourse's situational, overdetermined reality, our work (and this is a point I want to emphasize in this conclusion) is all the harder for its promise of indeterminacy and incompleteness.

It is the rare person who can bring an air of hopefulness and *joie de vivre* to an anti-foundational philosophy; the majority of theorists remain aloof from any discussion of its subjective effects. One exception can be found in the philosopher Cornell West, who, in the process of distinguishing himself from the Afro-centrist philosopher Molefi Asante, extols the pleasure he takes in his anti-foundationalism. He writes:

> [Asante] advocates a conception of self that is grounded in a unified field of African culture. But that way of framing the question is alien to me. I'm not for a solid anything. I begin with radical cultural hybridity, an improvisational New World sensibility. I always think that we are in process, making and remaking ourselves along the way. I see it in Louis Armstrong, I see it in Sarah Vaughan, I see it in Emerson's essays, I see it in Whitman's poetry about democratic vistas.
>
> I would point out to Asante that there is nothing wrong with affirming African humanity if we recognize that African civilizations, like European civilizations, have an ambiguous legacy—barbarism on the one hand and humanism on the other. . . . My aim is to keep those two motifs in my head at the same time. (Anderson, 1994: 48)

In these comments, West fashions a lively counter-discourse to foundationalism, a counter-discourse characterized by Foucault in terms of the following four principles: reversal, discontinuity, specificity, and exteriority. In the principle of reversal, we are reminded that as discourses are produced, so too they are also suppressed. As West suggests above, it is as important to identify the rules of a discourse's exclusion (e.g., regarding Africa's humanism) as a discourse's inclusion (e.g., regarding Africa's barbarism), and in this reversal from custom, Foucault's first principle is realized. In the principle of discontinuity, we are cautioned not to fall back on foundationalism when practicing reversal—in the manner of Asante's Afro-centrism. The restored discourse of Africa's humanism, in other words, is not more "true" or unified for having been suppressed. "[W]e must not imagine," Foucault writes, "some unsaid thing, or an unthought, floating about the world" (229). Instead, he argues what West demonstrates, that "Discourse must be treated as a discontinuous activity, its different manifestations sometimes coming together [as do, for instance, Ralph Waldo Emerson and Sarah Vaughan in West's statement] but just as easily unaware of, or excluding each other [as is customary with discussions of Emerson and Vaughan]" (229).

From these two principles follows the principle of specificity, which, as we have already seen, highlights the historicity and interestedness of discourse—including the discourse of Afro-centrism—seen by West as itself an event imposed on other events. As a specific reality, Afro-centrist discourse is itself formative. With the fourth principle, that of exteriority, we are reminded, as with the principle of discontinuity, not to revert to a new essentialism of the specific object. Discourse's external effects on the field of African studies, the conditions of its existence, are what we must study rather than looking for African culture's inner essence—what Foucault calls its "hidden core" (229) and West, its "unified field."

When we position ourselves to an area of study through the above four discursive practices—reversal, discontinuity, specificity, and exteriority—a conception of our own subjectivity as founded and centered may also begin to give way, as we see in West. Dispensed by our discursive relations "in a multiplicity of possible positions and functions" (231), we are the effects not only of cultural but also of discursive "hybridity." By way of conclusion, it remains to be seen in what ways these methodological principles and the conceptions of self they construct may actually serve the counterhegemonic literacy practices discussed in this book. After all, the fact that these principles dispense one in an ensemble of contradictory discourses would seem, at least at first glance, to compose a radically disarticulated, disempowered subject.

Indeed, Afro-centrist philosophers are not alone in their efforts to resist these anti-foundational principles and the cultural dispersion they threaten. Students also resist. In the case of Afro-centrists, we see an effort to thread the needle between the cultural losses implied by anti-foundationalism and the cultural domination implied by foundationalism. Replacing Euro-centrism with Afro-centrism, these philosophers opt for reversal *with* continuity: history is still centered, but the site is new. Only when the costs and limits of these solutions are strongly experienced will there be sufficient motive to push beyond them.

In the context of postsecondary education, it is increasingly apparent to those who teach literacy that the multileveled, conflict-ridden lives of many American college students leave them intellectually stranded in a field of contradictory discourses that they struggle to resolve through the unifying methods of the foundational systems they know. The social and personal ineffectuality of these resolutions take their toll, revealing the severely limited capacities of their literacies to address their situations. Even when the forms of these resolutions are technically literate, even moving, the incommensurability of a unifying discourse on the ensemble of competing and contradictory events involved stands out as such a problem of interpretation that one could be tempted to concur with those who profess that literacy *is* in crisis. Bound by the foundational systems of language and self, truth, and knowledge that they have not yet learned to problematize, students employ these outmoded foundational discourses to address startling arrays of contemporary social reality. Much of *Working Theory* has been devoted to analyzing and responding to this situation in a way that does not itself fall into the mixed practice of reversal with continuity: antifoundationalism as a new authoritative discourse.

Instead, I have argued that the study of student writing as specific discourse practices can teach us what our own "discourse on language" with out students must be. For instance, the prior discussion contains an assumption about the mutual exclusivity of foundationalist and anti-foundationalist discourses which the following student paper belies. In this paper, the student shows a facility with *both* these discourses. They appear to coexist—as long as anti-foundationalist discourse applies to the Third World other and foundationalist discourse to himself. Understanding the specific meaning of these discourses for him and the limits they impose gives us a strong, sobering experience of what Foucault means by the discontinuity of discourses—their "different manifestations" sometimes coming together in ways that confirm our conventional assumptions and in ways that do not. The specific relationships that students strike with these opposing discourses should determine our pedagogical responses to them in a way that opens up the space for discourse analysis between "thought and words" in our own reading.

In Chapter 3, I discussed a student paper by Rick L. that followed from a reading of "Our Time," a chapter in John Edgar Wideman's book, *Brothers and Keepers*. My purpose, in part, was to show the discontinuous ways the student was struggling toward more internally persuasive relations with the points of view he presented. The following student paper—which I will discuss in selected parts—is based on the same assignment, asking students to look at languages in terms of the points of view they construct. Specifically, students were asked to tell a story from their own point of view and at least one other, and then to discuss what they had learned about language, self, and experience as a result of having written from these different points of view.

In "What Do You Do?" Jeff L.,[1] a 22-year-old native English speaker from Memphis, tells a story related to his work as a missionary and translator in Haiti (the earlier religious work apparently creating the conditions for the later commercial work), on the basis of contacts he had made and the fluency with Haitian-Creole he had acquired. As a full-time student in Boston working as a translator for Haitian immigrants, local hospitals, and national journalists traveling to Haiti, Jeff had a wealth of experience to bring to the questions that Wideman raises about the specific power of language to shape points of view.

For his part, Jeff tells a story dramatic enough for popular cinema, and he gives it, if not a happy ending, a Hollywood ending nevertheless. In his story, he articulates a complex set of personal, social, and historical forces that have converged and now require him to make a monumental decision: Will he temporarily marry the sister of a Haitian friend and bring her to the United States so that she can escape further threats of rape and terror in Haiti?

Tracing his decision-making process through a consideration of five perspectives, Jeff discusses the points of view of (1) his father; (2) his mother; (3) his girlfriend, Selena; (4) his Haitian friend, Emmy; and (5) himself. In his impulse to fulfill Emmy's wish to save her sister through marriage, he associates the discourse of his father:

> My father was good at a lot of things but his ace was generosity. Kind of like Jesus when he took four loaves of bread and two fishes and fed thousands. My dad never had more than the equivalent of four loaves and two fishes but he also seemed to be able to give, and give on a large scale. . . . I wanted to be like dad. You know, do miracles like he did.

In his resistance to the idea of marrying Emmy's sister, he associates the disapproval of his girlfriend, Selena, with the more restrained temperament of his mother. His girlfriend, he imagines, would criticize him for making "stupid emotional decisions without thinking of all the consequences.... Marrying someone to get them into another country is illegal and dishonest." His mother, he tells us, similar to Selena, "was able to do her *part* . . . she would help others but only to a point."

In the way that he represents Emmy's needs in relation to his father's values, Jeff fashions a powerful discursive link between victim and savior, a linkage with many traditional sources. This linkage conflicts strongly with his representation of Selena's needs and his mother's values. This opposition between absolute and relative standards, as it is constructed by many layers of discourse on *each* side, provides a good example of what Foucault means by a "discourse event." As I discussed earlier, it is at the junctures of these events that the composer has the most work to do, teasing apart the discourses that are converging to form meanings in opposition. However, Jeff, having represented his experience in terms of these ensembles, is now stymied. As he turns thoughts into words, he does not see their assemblage by discourse. Worse yet for him, these ensembles, though oppositional, do not split into the customary binary opposition of right versus wrong that his system of knowledge has led him to expect. Instead, they split into absolute versus relative systems of knowledge, and this unexpected opposition confuses him.

When he eventually chooses against the absolute values of the helping father and makes a decision not to marry Emmy's sister, he is left with little to say about it—his foundational system of belief having failed to explain to him why he could not do right by his girlfriend *and* Emmy equally. Unable to work the theories that are working him, he is left with "unbearable" guilt and the sense that he "ended up upsetting everyone." In the end, he writes sadly, "I'll just have to find another way to work miracles." Having represented the relationships among five discourses—some of which are complementary, and others, as Selena's and Emmy's, contradictory—he is still looking for a central unifying discourse that will resolve them. For Jeff, it seems, a miracle worker is a translator who can find a universal discourse to reconcile all the competing realities he is part of. In identifying with his father and the Christian tradition he represents, Jeff retains the belief that he himself can mediate these competing systems of signification. The founding subject is construed here as missionary/translator: healer of dis-

Epilogue

course difference. In itself, the application of these traditional themes to his desperate situation is no surprise.

What is surprising and instructive about Jeff's paper is the way that this personal foundationalism coexists with a different discourse on Haiti with which he is also fluent. Were this discourse to be applied to himself, it might provide him with more insight regarding his choices for action than the statement, "I'll just have to find another way to work miracles." In other words, when it comes to consciousness about the discourses shaping his own subject position and the narrow range of actions they construct, Jeff is rather monologic and passive. However, the terse way in which he is able to insert *Emmy's* humanitarian efforts into a specific historical context, rife with brutal contradictions, suggests that, he is aware of the numerous motifs making and remaking Haiti in the present. In the following passage, Jeff provides a thumb-nail sketch of the situation in Haiti as he witnessed it in the fall of 1993, when Jean-Bertrand Aristide was prevented from returning to Haiti to assume the presidency:

> Things in Haiti were tough. Tough isn't the word, tragic! I had performed interpreting for several journalists who had flooded the country waiting for the return of President Aristide. Since nothing ever goes right or happens on time in that country, it was no surprise for me, anyway, when no one showed. What was unfortunate was that the miltary in an effort to intimidate and let its presence be known, left several dead bodies in strategic places to let everyone know this wasn't to be a smooth transition. This was all normal. Corruption everywhere. Not a legitimate business or organization in the country. Everyone was out for number one. Most times you couldn't even trust family. At one point or another you would probably be roped by a cousin or at least a friend of one of the living males. If anyone helped you get ahead to any degree, everyone else was jealous, in some cases to the point they would endanger your life or send someone else to. For reasons like these, sometimes it was all I could do to keep from throwing papers in the air, going back to Memphis, and never speaking a word of creole again.

In this passage, Jeff indicates that he has some understanding of the overdetermined effects of power on the entire fabric of Haitian society. Observing the semiotic use of dead bodies as a language of repression, he gives new meaning to Foucault's statement that discourse is "a violence we do to things." In addition, he is able to notice the relationships among military repression, economic corruption, and family breakdown. Eschewing a traditional discourse of the founding subject, for instance, he observes the shaping effects of Haitian repression on the character and behavior of "the living males." Interestingly, however, his jettisoning a foundational discourse in relation to the Haitian situation does not seem to inspire a critique of this discourse in relation to himself. It remains a privileged preserve—not to be worked by theory—at least in the context of this English paper, despite the fact that the Wideman selection directly challenges its retention.

In the paragraphs that follow, Jeff introduces Emmy, a "deaf Haitian lady who had taken care of me since I arrived in Boston." His representation of her point of view follows a clear statement of his understanding that "there were big problems in Haiti and that the lives of her sisters were in real danger." With this confirmation of Emmy's reading of the events in Haiti, he shifts to her voice. He tries to imagine her thoughts while she waits to find out what Jeff's response to her request will be.

> Well we'll see how well he does. . . . But how can this young white boy understand my situation? At least some of it. He's had it easy all his life. Never been abandon, or grown up with so much poverty and sickness around him that he considered killing himself. I'm desperate! I have two sisters in Haiti who will never have a chance unless they make it here. I know, I've lived in both! What I haven't told Jeff yet is why I need him right now. You see, I got a call from one of my sisters two hours ago. Last night someone tried to rape Francine again. I hate Haitians! If I didn't believe in God I would have shot somebody by now! Since my mom died and there aren't any males that I can trust, my sisters have been completely unprotected! I send them money so they can live but that only makes the situation worse. Now, they are two beautiful girls unpro-

tected, with money and food! In reality, not a good situation to be in Haiti.

This white boy can't understand . . . I can't tell him about the rape attempts because as bad as I hate Haitians, you can't talk about Haitian affairs with foreigners. I hope he feels just bad enough that he'll do it for me . . . I'm desperate, I haven't slept well in months. Something has to happen: Not bad Jeff, you seem to have a clue, even though we know that whites and blacks can't really love each other.

In this passage, Jeff imagines Emmy's thought process, using information that he represents as confidential to her. Blurring the boundaries between their discourses, he seems to have no trouble revealing in her voice that he knows more than she thinks he knows. Extending himself into Haitian culture, he shows himself able—as West is able—to hold *its* opposing motifs of barbarity and humanity in his head at the same time. Of this decentered discourse on Haitian society, one can imagine West responding, as Emmy: "Not bad, Jeff."

Tempted as he is to marry Francine and so to fulfill his ideal of "giving someone a life," Jeff is discouraged by the threat of rejection from his girlfriend and the persuasive reasoning she offers: "I'm not sure I could support someone who would have to lie as many times as it would be necessary to the INS in order to make it work. Marriage is . . . not something to toy with. The vows are binding and real. He would say 'I do' to someone else. I couldn't handle it."

Out of the Haitian context and back on the native turf of discourse universality with Selena, the principle of *nonspecificity* applies. This principle declares that one discourse of "vows" is identical to another discourse of "vows." Understandably, Jeff is stymied. To Selena's authoritative principle—which Foucault calls discourse universality—he has no answer. Jeff is not able to work the theory working this principle with the techniques of reversal, discontinuity, specificity, and exteriority with which he has begun to work his discourse on Haiti. Completely continuous with his centered notion of himself as a founding subject, Selena's assumption of discourse universality reinforces his own foundational assumptions. Unable, on these terms, to analyze the ensemble of contradictory discourses in which he is involved, he has only a limited range of actions available. Understandably, then, he reverts to the trope of the failed miracle worker. It has been my argument throughout this book that were he able to imagine how much more like the "living males" in Haitian society he is—as also a subject of specific cultural and discursive forces—he might have been able to begin a more complex dialogue with his girlfriend about the position he was in, about the shaping power of their discourses, the specific differences between "vows" in one signifying system and another, and even what alternatives there might be to construing Francine's fate solely in terms of Jeff saving her or not saving her.

Despite his facility with a discourse of situationality in regard to Haitians, he resituates himself in a foundational discourse in relation to Selena. By exploring this point at length, I have wanted to bring out once more the nonneutral nature of our discursive systems and the limits on knowledge and action they construct. In itself, however, the acquisition of a nonfoundational point of view is not enough. As we see, it can be split off and applied to the nonprivileged other, a Third World discourse for the powerless who alone are subjects of history. The discriminatory nature of this split is continuous with the impoverished discourse it leaves the writer for himself. Where Jeff looks to the next opportunity to work miracles, I am suggesting that his reading and writing education helps him to work *discourses*. In that way, perhaps his literacy will have a chance to catch up with his situation so that what actions he chooses to take against repression and what actions he chooses not to take may be part of a larger understanding—an understanding of the specific discursive and cultural reality he is part of as a critical subject of history.

NOTE

1. The names of the writer and his associates have been changed to retain anonymity.

Works Cited

Althusser, Louis. *For Marx.* Trans. Ben Brewster. London: Verso, 1979.
———. *Lenin and Philosophy and Other Essays.* Trans. Ben Brewster. New York: Monthly Review, 1971.
Althusser, Louis, and Etienne Balibar. *Reading Capital.* Trans. Ben Brewster. London: Verso, 1979.
Anderson, Jervis. "The Public Intellectual." *The New Yorker.* January 17, 1994: 39–48.
Aronowitz, Stanley, and Henry A.. Giroux. *Postmodern Education: Politics, Culture and Social Criticism.* Minneapolis: University of Minnesota Press, 1991.
Bakhtin, M. M. *The Dialogic Imagination.* Trans. Caryl Emerson and Michael Holquist. Austin: University of Texas Press, 1981.
Bartholomae, David, and Anthony Petrosky. *Ways of Reading: An Anthology for Writers.* New York: St. Martin's Press, 1987.
Berger, John. *About Looking.* New York: Pantheon, 1980.
Berlin, James. "Poststructuralism, Cultural Studies, and the Composition Classroom: Postmodern Theory in Practice." *Rhetoric Review* (Fall 1992): 16–33.
———. "Rhetoric and Ideology in the Writing Class." *College English* 50 (1988): 477–94.
———. *Rhetoric and Reality: Writing Instruction in American Colleges, 1900–1985.* Carbondale: Southern Illinois University Press, 1987.
Berthoff, Ann E. *The Making of Meaning: Metaphors, Models and Maxims for Writing Teachers.* Portsmouth, N.H.: Boynton/Cook, 1981.
———. "'Reading the World . . . Reading the Word': Paulo Freire's Pedagogy of Knowing." *Only Connect: Uniting Reading and Writing.*

Ed. Thomas Newkirk. Portsmouth, N.H.: Boynton/Cook, 1986. 119–30.

Bialostosky, Don H. "Liberal Education, Writing, and the Dialogic Self." *Contending with Words: Composition and Rhetoric in a Postmodern Age*. Ed. Patricia Harkin and John Schilb. New York: Modern Language Association, 1991. 11–22.

Bizzell, Patricia, "Marxist Ideas in Composition Studies." *Contending with Words: Composition and Rhetoric in a Postmodern Age*. Ed. Patricia Harkin and John Schilb. New York: Modern Language Association, 1991. 52–68.

Clifford, John. "The Subject in Discourse." *Contending with Words: Composition and Rhetoric in a Postmodern Age*. Ed. Patricia Harkin and John Schilb. New York: Modern Language Association, 1991. 38–51.

Coles, William E., Jr., and James Vopat. *What Makes Writing Good*. Lexington, Mass.: D.C. Heath, 1985.

Coward, Rosalind, and John Ellis. *Language and Materialism*. Boston: Routledge, 1977.

Emerson, Caryl. "The Outer Word and Inner Speech: Bakhtin, Vygotsky, and the Internalization of Language." *Critical Inquiry* 10 (1983): 245–64.

Faigley, Lester. "Competing Theories of Process: A Critique and a Proposal." *College English* 48 (1986): 527–42.

———. *Fragments of Rationality: Postmodernity and the Subject of Composition*. Pittsburgh: University of Pittsburgh Press, 1992.

———. "Judging Writing, Judging Selves." *College Composition and Communication* 40 (1989): 395–412.

Felman, Shoshana. "Psychoanalysis and Education: Teaching Terminable and Interminable." *Yale French Studies* 63 (1982): 21–44.

Fish, Stanley. *Doing What Comes Naturally: Change, Rhetoric and the Practice of Theory in Literary and Legal Studies*. Durham, N.C.: Duke University Press, 1989.

Foucault, Michel. *The Archaeology of Knowledge*. Trans. A. M. Sheridan Smith. New York: Pantheon, 1972a.

———. *Discipline and Punish: The Birth of the Prison*. Trans. A. M. Sheridan Smith. New York: Pantheon, 1972b.

———. *Power/Knowledge: Selected Interviews and Other Writings, 1972–1977*. Ed. and trans. Colin Gordon. New York: Pantheon. 1980.

Freire, Paulo. *Pedagogy of the Oppressed*. Trans. Myra Bergman Ramos. New York: Seabury Press, 1968.

Freire, Paulo, and Donaldo Macedo. *Literacy: Reading the World and the Word*. South Hadley, Mass.: Bergin & Garvey, 1987.

Works Cited

Giroux, Henry. *Theory and Resistance in Education: A Pedagogy for the Opposition.* South Hadley, Mass.: Edward Arnold, 1978.

Graff, Harvey. *The Legacies of Literacy: Continuity and Contradictions in Western Culture and Society.* Bloomington: Indiana University Press, 1987.

―――. *The Literacy Myth: Literacy and Social Structure in a Nineteenth Century City.* New York: Academic Press, 1979.

Hairston, Maxine C. "The Winds of Change: Thomas Kuhn and the Revolution in the Teaching of Writing." *College Composition and Communication* 33 (1982): 76–88.

Jameson, Fredric. *Marxism and Form.* Princeton, N.J.: Princeton University Press, 1974.

―――. *The Political Unconscious.* New York: Cornell University Press, 1981.

Kingston, Maxine Hong. *The Woman Warrior: Memoirs of a Girlhood Among Ghosts.* New York: Vintage, 1977.

Knoblauch, C. H. "Rhetorical Constructions: Dialogue and Commitment." *College English* 50 (1988): 125–40.

Knoper, Randall. "Deconstruction, Process, Writing." *Reclaiming Pedagogy: The Rhetoric of the Classroom.* Ed. Patricia Donahue and Ellen Quandahl. Carbondale: Southern Illinois University Press, 1989. 128–43.

Kozol, Jonathon. "The Homeless and Their Children, I." *The New Yorker,* January 25, 1988: 65–71.

―――. "The Homeless and Their Children, II." *The New Yorker,* February 1, 1988: 36–44.

Kramer, Lynn. "Response." *College Composition and Communication* 43 (1922): 528–29.

Marx, Karl, and Friedrich Engels. *The German Ideology.* Ed. R. Pascal. New York: International: 1947.

Miller, J. Hillis. "Composition and Decomposition." *Composition and Literature: Bridging the Gap.* Ed. Winifred Bryan Horner. Chicago: University of Chicago Press, 1983. 38–56.

Miller, Susan. "Comment." *College English* 52 (1990): 330–34.

―――. *Rescuing the Subject: A Critical Introduction to Rhetoric and the Writer.* Carbondale: Southern Illinois University Press, 1989.

―――. *Textual Carnivals: The Politics of Composition.* Carbondale: Southern Illinois University Press, 1991.

Ohmann, Richard. *English in America: A Radical View of the Profession.* New York: Oxford University Press, 1976.

―――. "Preface." *Politics of Writing Instruction: Postsecondary.* Ed. Richard Bullock and John Trimbur. Portsmouth, N.H.: Boynton/Cook, 1991. ix–xvi.

Recchio, Thomas. "A Bakhtinian Reading of Student Writing." *College Composition and Communication* 42 (1991): 446–54.
Rodriguez, Richard. *Hunger of Memory: The Education of Richard Rodriguez.* Boston: Godine, 1981.
Rose, Mike. *Lives on the Boundary: The Struggles and Achievements of America's Underprepared.* New York: Free Press, 1989.
Sale, Roger. *On Writing.* New York: Random House, 1970.
Spellmeyer, Kurt. *Common Ground: Dialogue, Understanding and the Teaching of Composition.* Englewood Cliffs, N.J.: Prentice-Hall, 1993.
Trimbur, John. "Literacy and the Discourse of Crisis." *Politics of Writing Instruction: Postsecondary.* Ed. Richard Bullock and John Trimbur. Portsmouth, N.H.: Boynton/Cook, 1991. 277–95.
Tweedie, Sanford. "Response." *College Composition and Communication* 43 (1992): 526–28.
Vitanza, Victor J. "Three Countertheses: Or, A Critical In(ter)vention into Composition Theories and Pedagogies." *Contending with Words: Composition and Rhetoric in a Postmodern Age.* Ed. Patricia Harkin and John Schilb. New York: Modern Language Association, 1991. 139–72.
Wallace, Douglas. "Rhetoric for the Meritocracy." In Richard Ohmann, *English in America: A Radical View of the Profession.* New York: Oxford University Press, 1976.
Weimann, Robert. *Structure and Society in Literary History.* Charlottesville: University Press of Virginia, 1976.
White, Edward M. "Post-Structural Literary Criticism and the Response to Student Writing." *College Composition and Communication* 35 (1984): 186–95.
Williams, Raymond. *Marxism and Literature.* Oxford: Oxford University Press, 1977.

Index

About Looking (Berger), 26–30, 33–35
Afro-centrism, 125-26, 127
Althusser, Louis: Marxian perspective on reading and writing, 11–22; structural causality theory, 14–21
Anti-foundationalism, and Fish's argument against theory hope, 94–99
Aronowitz, Stanley, 88–89
Authoritative discourse, as negative dialogics, 43–47, 54–55, 59

Bakhtin, Mikhail, 43, 59, 83; "relativized consciousness" concept, 8, 45–47, 124; theory of language, 43–49, 71–72
Before-and-after personal narrative, 74, 84
Berger, John, 26–30, 33–35; concept of "radial knowledge," 116, 118–19
Berlin, James, 86, 114, 115
Berthoff, Ann, 24–25
Bizzell, Patricia, 100

Border pedagogy, 89–90

Coles, Robert, 58
Composition studies, 11–41; before-and-after personal narrative, 74, 84; "composition" versus "writing," 6; confessional narrative, 2, 51; dialectic method of composing, 24–26; freshman composition as "not-literature," 105; Harvard model, 66, 104–5; hegemonic discourse in, 68–69, 84–85, 109; narrative of loss, 75–76; product versus process models in, 22–24; revision assignments in, 55, 56–57; sequenced assignments in, 48–49, 51, 62, 120; theme writing, 69; traditional values in, 5–6, 111. *See also* Critical pedagogy; Essay
Conscientization, process of, 24–25, 28
Counterhegemonic practice. *See* Critical practice

Credentialing, reading and writing as, 103–5
Critical effectivity theory, 18–22; and Bakhtin's philosophy of language, 44; and critical nonidentity, 8, 31, 89–90, 93; and historicity, 66–71; implications for composition pedagogy, 26–41; principles of, 21–22, 26–27; and social contradictions, 31; subjectivity in, 18, 38–39
Critical pedagogy, 108–22; foundational premises in, 108–9, 111; informed by internally persuasive discourse, 46–47; overdetermination and contradiction in, 18, 67–68, 99–101; process of critical effectivity in, 26–41; process-centered, 22–24, 105–6, 112; residual and emergent elements in, 112–13; reterritorialization concept in, 41, 43; rhetoric in, 108–9; in structural causality theory, 18–22; students as researchers in, 108; teacher's role in, 63–65

Darwin, Charles, 3
Determination/overdetermination concepts, 67–68
Dialectic(s): dialectic of composing, 24; dialectical self-consciousness, 24–26; dialectical thinking, 29, 31–32, 65; as formalist problem solving, 33; Hegelian, 16–17, 25; Marxian, 11–22, 25, 100; and social contradictions, 31–32
Dialogic Imagination, The (Bakhtin), 43
Dialogism: and critical interanimation, 47–48, 115, 119, 120; and dialogic action, 43–44, 48–49, 51, 62; dialogic forms, 65–67; and heteroglossia, 44–45, 47, 115; and relativized consciousness, 44–45
Discourse(s): discourse event, 130; discourse specificity, principle of, 123–28; and founding subject, 125, 130–31; hegemonic, 48–49, 60, 68–69, 84–85, 109; toward internally persuasive relations, 43–62; opposing, 48–49, 50–51, 57, 128; recontextualization in, 48–49, 60; structuring effects of, 76–77, 85; universality concept, 123, 133; university discourse relations, 76–77. *See also* Internally persuasive discourse

Eagleton, Terry, 23
Educational ideological state appartus (Althusser), 18–22
Essay form: and Bakhtin's dialogic model of consciousness, 72–73; and concepts of overdetermination/determination, 67–68; conjunctural effects in, 8; as dialogic form, 65, 67; historical contraints, 66–68; and Montaigne, 65–66; and situated knowledge, 66–67

Faigley, Lester, 74–76
Fish, Stanley, 8, 93; argument against anti-foundationalist theory hope, 94–99
Foucault, Michel, 82, 130, 133; principle of discourse specificity, 123–28; specific versus universal intellectual, 1–6, 123–24

Index

Foundationalist ideology, 94–96, 99, 101
Freire, Paulo, 24, 65, 100; teacher-student concept, 63–64, 90

Gadamer, Hans Georg, 89
Giroux, Henry, 19, 89
Gramsci, Antonio, 21, 101

Hairston, Maxine, 22–23
Hegemonic discourse relations, 22, 68–69, 84–85, 109. *See also* Counterhegemonic practice
Hegemony, cultural: and language, 29; and literacy, 101–4
Heteroglossia, 44–45, 47, 115
Hirsh, E. D., 96
Historical materialism, pedagogical function of, 17–18
Historicity: and concept of determination/overdetermination, 72–73, 99–100; in critical effectivity theory, 66–71; dialectical approach to, 99; in Marxian dialectic, 13–16; and negative dialogics, 72–73; reification of concept, 71; and subjectivity, 66–71

Idealist epistemologies, Marx's challenge to, 13–14
Ideology: ideological analysis, 17–18; ideological becoming, 44, 49, 50–51, 88–89; ideological recognition, mechanisms for, 20–21, 33–39, 41; in materialist epistemologies, 14–18; as practice of representation, 17–18; resistance to, 18–19
Interanimation: of conflicting discourses, 48–49, 50–51, 57; critical, 47–48, 115, 119, 120; and ideological becoming, 50–51

Internally persuasive discourse, Bakhtin's concept of: versus authoritative discourse, 46–47, 50; and concept of overdetermination, 18, 67–68, 99–101; recontextualization and interanimation in, 48–49

Jameson, Fredric, 16, 31

Knoper, Randall, 98
Knowledge: foundational-values versus use-values in, 101; idealist theories of, 13–14; production of, 13–14; in structural causality theory, 14–18; transcendent, 5, 14
Kozol, Jonathon, 77, 87

Language(s): assumptions, and course structuring, 74–75; Bakhtin's theory of, 43–49, 71–72; heteroglossia and dialogism in, 44–45, 47, 115; interanimation, 99–101; social code and individual message dichotomy, 47–48; and social psyche development, 47–48; social nature of, 44. *See also* Discourse
Literacy: and cultural hegemony, 101–4; and rhetoric, 120–22; schooled, 101–3

Marx, Karl, 11
Marxist dialectic, implications for reading and writing, 11–22, 25, 100
Materialist epistemologies, 14–18; ideology as material force in, 17–18
Miller, J. Hillis, 97–98
Miller, Susan, 22, 23–24, 66–67, 68, 93, 104–6

Negative dialogics: authoritative discourse as, 43–47, 54–55; generative power of, 54–55; and historicity, 72–73

Ohmann, Richard, 69–70, 77, 83, 84, 85, 86, 87, 89, 109
Oppenheimer, J. Robert, 3
Overdetermination and contradiction, 18, 67–68, 99–101

Perspectivism, as denaturing process, 100
Process pedagogy, 22–24; critique of, 105–6; versus product-centered model, 22–23; traditional forms of student subjectivity in, 112

Reader-response theory, 114
Reading: as credentialing device, 103–5; Marxian perspective on, 11–22. See also Composition studies; Writing
Recchio, Thomas, 49–50
Recontextualization, in critical discourse, 48–49, 60
Relativized consciousness, Bakhtin's concept of, 8, 45–47, 124
Reterritorialization, 41, 43
Revision assignments, 55, 56–57
Rhetoric: and anti-foundationalism, 94; and counterhegemonic practice, 108–9; current-traditional, 86, 89; and historical moment, 114–15; and teacher-student relations, 114–15, 121–22

Schooled literacy, 101–3
Sequenced assignments, 62, 120; and dialogic action, 48–49, 51

Situationality: and concept of critical effectivity, 99–101; contradictions and overdetermination in, 72–73, 99–101; paradox of teaching, 99
Social construction of meaning, 25
Social psyche, individual psyche as, 72
Specific intellectual, Foucault's concept of, 1–6, 123–24
Specificity, Foucault's principle of, 123, 126–27
Spellmeyer, Kurt, 63–66, 89
Structural causality, Althusser's theory of, 14–22; and concept of critical effectivity, 18–22; and subjectivity in academic discourse, 66–71
Subjectivity: in critical effectivity theory, 18, 38–39; and dialectic of identity/nonidentity, 90; and historicity, 66–71; as receiver's subjectivity, 70; self-knowledge of, 18

Teacher: as active historical subject, 115; in critical practice, 63–65, 90, 113; as maieutic dialectician, 63–64; as master reader of universal truth, 2–3; and role of rhetoric, 114–15, 121–22; as teacher-student, 63–64, 90. See also Critical practice
Theory and practice: dialectical interaction of, 114–15; Fish's argument against theory hope, 94–99
Transcendental subject concept, 14
Trimbur, John, 101–4

Universal intellectual, Foucault's concept of, 3–5

Vitazna, Victor, 113–14

West, Cornell, 125–26
Wheatley, Phillis, 111
Wideman, John Edgar, 52
Williams, Raymond, 112
Writing: as credentialing device, 103–5; as cultural artifact, 21, 26, 40; and decontextualized processes, 105–6; foundationalist notions of good writing, 95–99, 104; good writing, and assumptions about language, 74–76; "how to write/what to write" relationship, 96–97; and rhetoric, 97, 120–21; theory, anti-foundationalist versus foundationalist, 94–88; "timeless value" assumptions, 106, 107. *See also* Composition studies

About the Author

JUDITH GOLEMAN is Associate Professor of English at the University of Massachusetts, Boston, where she directs the Freshman English Program and the Graduate Intern Program in composition.

www.ingramcontent.com/pod-product-compliance
Lightning Source LLC
Chambersburg PA
CBHW070333230426
43663CB00011B/2299